ACCOUNTING LIFE
PAYROLL RECOR

MW00800008

CONTENTS

Author: Daniel L. Ritzman, B.S.
Editors: Alan Christopherson, M.S.
                     Jennifer L. Davis, B.S.

ALPHA OMEGA
PUBLICATIONS

300 North McKemy Avenue, Chandler, Arizona 85226-2618

ACCOUNTING LIFEPAC 8
PAYROLL RECORDS

OVERVIEW

Payroll accounting is a very important function of every business that hires employees. Handling payroll involves much more than recording the payroll transactions and paying cash to employees. It also requires accounting for: (1) withholdings from employees' **wages**, (2) employer payroll taxes, and (3) employee benefits programs maintained by the employer.

The purpose of this LIFEPAC is to provide an understanding of the payroll process and responsibilities.

OBJECTIVES

When you have completed this LIFEPAC you will be able to:

1. Define accounting terms associated with payroll records;

2. Understand accounting practices used to maintain payroll records;

3. List the mandatory and voluntary deductions that are withheld from employee wages;

4. List the major benefits of the Social Security program;

5. Analyze a time card;

6. Calculate gross wages;

7. Prepare a payroll register;

8. Make the necessary calculations to the payroll register; and

9. Complete an employee earnings record.

VOCABULARY

Study + Learn

Employee Earnings Record – a form used to summarize payroll payments made to each individual employee.

Federal Unemployment Tax (FUTA) – a federal tax used for administration of state and federal unemployment programs.

Federal Insurance Contribution Act (FICA) – a law requiring employers and employees to pay taxes to the federal government to support the Social Security programs; "FICA" also refers to the taxes themselves.

Gross Earnings – the total amount due each employee for the pay period before any payroll deductions; also referred to as gross pay.

Pay Period – a period covered by a salary payment.

Payroll – all salaries and wages paid to employees.

Payroll Deductions – required and voluntary deductions from gross earnings to determine net pay.

Payroll Register – an accounting form that summarizes payroll information for all employees during a specific pay period.

Quarterly – every three months; in a calendar year the quarters are January through March, April through June, July through September and October through December.

Salary – a payment plan that pays employees a fixed amount for each pay period.

Semimonthly – twice a month; refers to a pay period that usually falls on the 15th and the 31st of the month.

State Unemployment Tax – a tax imposed by a state to pay benefits to the unemployed.

Time and a Half – a term used to describe the rate a worker is paid for overtime. The overtime rate is the worker's regular hourly rate ("time") plus half his regular rate ("and a half").

Wages – payment based on an hourly rate or a piecework basis.

Withholding Allowance – the number of persons legally supported by the taxpayer.

SECTION I. PAYROLL FUNCTIONS & DEDUCTIONS

Payroll Functions

Payroll and related payroll taxes, along with employee benefits plans, constitute a major portion of a company's liabilities. In addition, employee compensation is often the largest expense that a company incurs. Since many businesses today are service-oriented, employee compensation is the major expense.

For this reason, it is important to note that payroll accounting is much more than recording transactions. Companies are required to maintain payroll records for each employee, file payroll taxes and comply with all federal and state employment regulations.

Payroll includes all salaries and wages paid to employees. Many managers, administrative personnel, and professional employees are paid a stated salary. A **salary** is paid as a specified amount per month or per year based upon the employee's contract. Normally clerks, factory employees and manual laborers are paid wages. **Wages** paid are based on an hourly rate or a piecework basis. It is common practice to use the words *salaries* and *wages* interchangeably.

A company's payroll procedures include the following three functions:

1. Hiring employees,
2. Timekeeping, and
3. Preparing and paying the payroll.

Larger companies have found it to their advantage to assign each of these functions to a different department or a different employee in the payroll department. In smaller companies, a single payroll clerk usually carries out these functions.

Hiring Employees. The listing of job openings, carrying out the screening process, interviewing the applicants and hiring employees is the responsibility of the owner, manager or the human resources (personnel) department. These people must inform the payroll department or payroll clerk that an individual has been hired and needs to be placed on the payroll.

The owner, manager or human resources department also authorizes pay rate changes and terminations of employees. The changes are made in accordance with the employee contract or a union contract. The changes should be in writing and sent to the proper individual or department required to make payments.

Timekeeping. Inaccurate timekeeping could cost a business large sums of money; therefore, it is very important to control the timekeeping process. Hourly employees should be required to "punch" a time card to record time worked. By punching in on a time clock, time of arrival and departure are automatically recorded when the employee's time card is inserted into the time clock.

Time clock procedures vary by the size of the business. Many businesses provide a security guard to make sure an employee uses only one card. In other businesses the time clock is monitored by the payroll clerk or manager. At the end of the **pay period**, a period covered by a salary or wage payment, the employee and the employee's supervisor must sign the time card to verify the hours worked. All overtime hours must be approved by the supervisor or manger in order to keep overtime costs under control. For salaried employees, a manually-prepared time report is generally used as a record of time worked.

Preparing and Paying the Payroll. A payroll is prepared by the payroll department or payroll clerk based on two sources of information: (1) payroll rate authorizations, and (2) approved and verified time cards. It is the payroll clerk's responsibility to calculate the gross wages and **payroll deductions**. The payroll clerk prepares the payroll checks, maintains payroll records and prepares payroll tax returns.

The payroll is paid by the accounting department. Payment is usually made by check to reduce the risk of loss, and the endorsed payroll check is evidence of payment. All checks must be signed by the owner or his/her agent. This agent may be a bookkeeper, treasurer or business manager.

Mandatory Payroll Deductions

If you receive a paycheck, you know that your **gross earnings** are greater than the amount you actually receive. The difference is due to payroll deductions. **Payroll deductions** are deductions from gross earnings to determine net pay. Some payroll deductions are mandatory and others are voluntary.

Social Security Taxes (FICA). The Social Security Act, enacted in 1935 by President Roosevelt, created a Social Security Board (SSB). Its function was to administer the new act. Its first responsibility was to assign a Social Security number to each employee in the United States. Its other functions included administering and distributing retirement payments.

Later the SSB became the SSA (Social Security Administration), responsible for enforcing the new laws under the modified Social Security Act. The administration was originally part of the Federal Security Agency but became an independent agency in 1995.

The **Federal Insurance Contribution Act (FICA)** requires employers and employees to pay taxes (FICA taxes) to the federal government to support the Social Security programs.

Employees can receive the following benefits from the Social Security Administration if they are eligible.

1. *Retirement Benefits.* The Social Security Act provides that qualified workers who reach the age of 62 and retire shall receive monthly retirement benefits for the remainder of their lives. The amount of benefits depends upon age at retirement. If you retire at age 62 you will receive less than retiring at 65 or older.

2. *Disability Benefits.* Any worker who becomes disabled on the job can collect Social Security benefits, no matter what their age. There is, however, a minimum contribution to the system before the employee is disabled. If the employee did not contribute the minimum into Social Security, he is not eligible for benefits. Disability payments are also made to the spouse and dependent children of the disabled worker.

3. *Survivor's Benefits.* The Social Security Administration usually pays benefits to the spouse with dependent children of a worker who dies. The monthly benefits received by the survivors are a percentage of the amount the worker would have received. The percentage is determined in part by whether the worker is employed and the number of dependent children. Dependent children of a retired, disabled or deceased worker usually receive a monthly benefit until they reach the age of 18. A surviving spouse without dependent children is not eligible for survivor's benefits until he or she reaches the age of 60.

4. *Medicare Benefits.* A major portion of Social Security funds is used to support the Medicare Insurance program. The Social Security funds, under Medicare provisions, provide federal hospital insurance for people who are over 65 or are disabled. To be eligible for Medicare, the worker must be eligible for Social Security benefits or railroad retirement benefits.

Each eligible employee must contribute to FICA. The contribution is based on gross earnings. The contribution rate for Social Security is 6.2% at the present time. The tax rate is applied to the first $76,200.00 of wages earned. The self-employed person is subject to 12.4% of the first $76,200.00 of the net profit of the business.

The Medicare tax rate is 1.45% of gross earnings. The Medicare tax must be paid on all salaries and wages earned. Congress has removed the dollar limit for Medicare contributions. The self-employed individual is subject to a 2.9% tax on net profits.

5

In addition to the employee being liable for Social Security payments, the employer must contribute to the funds at the same rate as the employee. Therefore, the employer must pay 6.2% for FICA tax and 1.45% for Medicare tax on each employee's total earnings.

By using this method of collecting contributions, the employee and employer contribute 12.4% to an employee's Social Security fund and 2.9% to an employee's Medicare fund. The basic theory of Social Security is to have the employee and employer contribute to a retirement plan for each eligible worker.

Federal Income Taxes. Under federal law, employers are required to withhold income from their employees' wages. The amount to be withheld depends upon three variables: (1) gross earnings, (2) the number of allowances claimed by the employee, and (3) the pay period.

1. "Gross earnings" refers to the total amount of compensation received for the pay period before deductions are made. The compensation includes wages/salary, bonuses, tips and commissions.

2. The number of allowances is based on two factors: (1) marital status – married or single, and (2) **withholding allowance** – the number of persons legally supported by the taxpayer. To inform the employer of each of these factors, the employee must prepare a W-4 form (Employee's Withholding Allowance Certificate). A sample W-4 form is shown below.

Form **W-4** Department of the Treasury Internal Revenue Service	**Employee's Withholding Allowance Certificate** ► For Privacy Act and Paperwork Reduction Act Notice, see page 2.	OMB No. 1545-0010 **2000**

1 Type or print your first name and middle initial *Gertrude A.*	Last name *Schwartz*	2 Your social security number *123 45 6789*
Home address (number and street or rural route) *456 Miscellaneous Street*	3 ☒ Single ☐ Married ☐ Married, but withhold at higher Single rate. **Note:** If married, but legally separated, or spouse is a nonresident alien, check the Single box.	
City or town, state, and ZIP code *Anytown, US 12345*	4 If your last name differs from that on your social security card, check here. **You must call 1-800-772-1213 for a new card** . . . ► ☐	

5	Total number of allowances you are claiming (from line **H** above **OR** from the applicable worksheet on page 2)	**5** *1*
6	Additional amount, if any, you want withheld from each paycheck	**6** $
7	I claim exemption from withholding for 2000, and I certify that I meet **BOTH** of the following conditions for exemption:	
	● Last year I had a right to a refund of **ALL** Federal income tax withheld because I had **NO** tax liability **AND**	
	● This year I expect a refund of **ALL** Federal income tax withheld because I expect to have **NO** tax liability.	
	If you meet both conditions, write "EXEMPT" here . . . . ►	**7**

Under penalties of perjury, I certify that I am entitled to the number of withholding allowances claimed on this certificate, or I am entitled to claim exempt status.
Employee's signature
(Form is not valid unless you sign it) ► *Gertrude A. Schwartz*   Date ► *4-22-00*

8 Employer's name and address (Employer: Complete lines 8 and 10 only if sending to the IRS.)	9 Office code (optional)	10 Employer identification number

Cat. No. 10220Q

3. Pay periods can be weekly, biweekly (every other week), **semimonthly** (twice a month— usually the 1st and the 15th), and monthly. The federal government supplies withholding tables that determine the amount of tax to be withheld. These withholding amounts are based on gross earnings and the number of allowances claimed. The greater the number of allowances, the smaller the tax that is withheld.

The payroll clerk determines the amount of income tax withholding for an employee by using a withholding table like the one pictured on the next page.

For example, a married employee with 3 exemptions has total earnings in a weekly pay period of $645.00.

6

1. Locate the proper earnings level on the tax table. If gross wages are $645.00, locate the line that says **At least $640 – But less than $650**.

2. Find the column that has the correct number of withholding allowances claimed: **3**.

3. Find the withholding amount: **$54.00**. This amount is entered in the payroll register in the Federal Income Tax column. (The payroll register will be discussed further in Section III.)

MARRIED Persons- **WEEKLY** Payroll Period
(For Wages Paid in 2000)

If the wages are-		And the number of withholding allowances claimed is-										
At least	But less than	0	1	2	3	4	5	6	7	8	9	10
		The amount of income tax to be withheld is-										
$0	$125	0	0	0	0	0	0	0	0	0	0	0
125	130	1	0	0	0	0	0	0	0	0	0	0
130	135	1	0	0	0	0	0	0	0	0	0	0
135	140	2	0	0	0	0	0	0	0	0	0	0
140	145	3	0	0	0	0	0	0	0	0	0	0
145	150	4	0	0	0	0	0	0	0	0	0	0
150	155	4	0	0	0	0	0	0	0	0	0	0
155	160	5	0	0	0	0	0	0	0	0	0	0
160	165	6	0	0	0	0	0	0	0	0	0	0
165	170	7	0	0	0	0	0	0	0	0	0	0
170	175	7	0	0	0	0	0	0	0	0	0	0
175	180	8	0	0	0	0	0	0	0	0	0	0
180	185	9	1	0	0	0	0	0	0	0	0	0
185	190	10	1	0	0	0	0	0	0	0	0	0
190	195	10	2	0	0	0	0	0	0	0	0	0
195	200	11	3	0	0	0	0	0	0	0	0	0
200	210	12	4	0	0	0	0	0	0	0	0	0
210	220	14	6	0	0	0	0	0	0	0	0	0
220	230	15	7	0	0	0	0	0	0	0	0	0
230	240	17	9	0	0	0	0	0	0	0	0	0
240	250	18	10	2	0	0	0	0	0	0	0	0
250	260	20	12	3	0	0	0	0	0	0	0	0
260	270	21	13	5	0	0	0	0	0	0	0	0
270	280	23	15	6	0	0	0	0	0	0	0	0
280	290	24	16	8	0	0	0	0	0	0	0	0
290	300	26	18	9	1	0	0	0	0	0	0	0
300	310	27	19	11	3	0	0	0	0	0	0	0
310	320	29	21	12	4	0	0	0	0	0	0	0
320	330	30	22	14	6	0	0	0	0	0	0	0
330	340	32	24	15	7	0	0	0	0	0	0	0
340	350	33	25	17	9	1	0	0	0	0	0	0
350	360	35	27	18	10	2	0	0	0	0	0	0
360	370	36	28	20	12	4	0	0	0	0	0	0
370	380	38	30	21	13	5	0	0	0	0	0	0
380	390	39	31	23	15	7	0	0	0	0	0	0
390	400	41	33	24	16	8	0	0	0	0	0	0
400	410	42	34	26	18	10	2	0	0	0	0	0
410	420	44	36	27	19	11	3	0	0	0	0	0
420	430	45	37	29	21	13	5	0	0	0	0	0
430	440	47	39	30	22	14	6	0	0	0	0	0
440	450	48	40	32	24	16	8	0	0	0	0	0
450	460	50	42	33	25	17	9	1	0	0	0	0
460	470	51	43	35	27	19	11	3	0	0	0	0
470	480	53	45	36	28	20	12	4	0	0	0	0
480	490	54	46	38	30	22	14	6	0	0	0	0
490	500	56	48	39	31	23	15	7	0	0	0	0
500	510	57	49	41	33	25	17	9	1	0	0	0
510	520	59	51	42	34	26	18	10	2	0	0	0
520	530	60	52	44	36	28	20	12	4	0	0	0
530	540	62	54	45	37	29	21	13	5	0	0	0
540	550	63	55	47	39	31	23	15	7	0	0	0
550	560	65	57	48	40	32	24	16	8	0	0	0
560	570	66	58	50	42	34	26	18	10	2	0	0
570	580	68	60	51	43	35	27	19	11	3	0	0
580	590	69	61	53	45	37	29	21	13	5	0	0
590	600	71	63	54	46	38	30	22	14	6	0	0
600	610	72	64	56	48	40	32	24	16	8	0	0
610	620	74	66	57	49	41	33	25	17	9	1	0
620	630	75	67	59	51	43	35	27	19	11	2	0
630	640	77	69	60	52	44	36	28	20	12	4	0
640	650	78	70	62	54	46	38	30	22	14	5	0
650	660	80	72	63	55	47	39	31	23	15	7	0
660	670	81	73	65	57	49	41	33	25	17	8	0
670	680	83	75	66	58	50	42	34	26	18	10	2
680	690	84	76	68	60	52	44	36	28	20	11	3
690	700	86	78	69	61	53	45	37	29	21	13	5
700	710	87	79	71	63	55	47	39	31	23	14	6
710	720	89	81	72	64	56	48	40	32	24	16	8
720	730	90	82	74	66	58	50	42	34	26	17	9
730	740	92	84	75	67	59	51	43	35	27	19	11

Page 38

7

✴ **State Income Taxes.** States and cities may also impose income taxes on employees. If such taxes are imposed, the employer is required to withhold them also. The withholding procedure is the same as the federal government, using the same criteria. The state and city supplies the withholding tax tables and the employer determines the tax to be withheld. The basis for withholdings is: (1) gross earnings, (2) the number of allowances, and (3) the pay period.

In some states, the income tax is figured using a percentage of the employee's federal withholding amount. Other states use a tax table similar to the one shown below:

ANNUAL WAGE BRACKET WITHHOLDING TABLE
IF THE PAYROLL PERIOD WITH RESPECT TO AN EMPLOYEE IS ANNUAL

AND THE WAGES ARE — AND THE NUMBER OF WITHHOLDING EXEMPTIONS CLAIMED IS-

AT LEAST	BUT LESS THAN	0	1	2	3	4	5	6	7	8 OR MORE
		THE AMOUNT OF STATE INCOME TAX TO BE WITHHELD SHALL BE—								
$ 0.	$ 1,000.	$ 0	$ 0	$ 0	$ 0	$ 0	$ 0	$ 0	$ 0	$ 0
1,000.	2,000.	0	0	0	0	0	0	0	0	0
2,000.	3,000.	4	0	0	0	0	0	0	0	0
3,000.	4,000.	10	0	0	0	0	0	0	0	0
4,000.	5,000.	32	12	0	0	0	0	0	0	0
5,000.	6,000.	56	36	0	0	0	0	0	0	0
6,000.	7,000.	97	78	0	0	0	0	0	0	0
7,000.	8,000.	139	126	14	0	0	0	0	0	0
8,000.	9,000.	180	175	53	13	0	0	0	0	0
9,000.	10,000.	221	221	102	62	22	0	0	0	0
10,000.	11,000.	263	262	150	110	70	30	0	0	0
11,000.	12,000.	304	304	199	159	119	79	39	0	0
12,000.	13,000.	351	357	243	207	167	127	87	47	7
13,000.	14,000.	407	413	284	258	218	178	138	98	58
14,000.	15,000.	462	468	338	324	284	244	204	164	124
15,000.	16,000.	518	524	393	380	349	309	269	229	189
16,000.	17,000.	573	579	449	435	414	374	334	294	254
17,000.	18,000.	629	635	504	491	477	440	400	360	320
18,000.	19,000.	684	690	560	546	533	505	465	425	385
19,000.	20,000.	740	747	615	602	588	570	530	490	450
20,000.	22,000.	828	836	699	686	674	662	633	593	553
22,000.	24,000.	946	955	816	804	793	781	769	733	693
24,000.	26,000.	1,065	1,073	935	923	911	900	888	873	833
26,000.	28,000.	1,186	1,196	1,054	1,042	1,030	1,020	1,011	1,001	980
28,000.	30,000.	1,314	1,324	1,177	1,167	1,158	1,148	1,138	1,129	1,119
30,000.	32,000.	1,442	1,452	1,305	1,295	1,285	1,276	1,266	1,257	1,247
32,000.	34,000.	1,569	1,580	1,432	1,423	1,413	1,404	1,394	1,385	1,375
34,000.	36,000.	1,697	1,708	1,560	1,551	1,541	1,532	1,522	1,512	1,503
36,000.	38,000.	1,825	1,835	1,688	1,678	1,669	1,659	1,650	1,640	1,631
38,000.	40,000.	1,953	1,964	1,816	1,806	1,797	1,787	1,778	1,771	1,765
40,000.	42,000.	2,093	2,107	1,944	1,938	1,932	1,926	1,920	1,914	1,909
42,000.	44,000.	2,236	2,250	2,087	2,081	2,075	2,069	2,063	2,058	2,052
44,000.	46,000.	2,379	2,393	2,230	2,224	2,218	2,213	2,207	2,201	2,195
46,000.	48,000.	2,519	2,536	2,373	2,367	2,362	2,356	2,350	2,344	2,338
48,000.	50,000.	2,641	2,679	2,517	2,511	2,505	2,499	2,493	2,487	2,481
50,000.	52,000.	2,762	2,805	2,660	2,654	2,648	2,642	2,636	2,630	2,624
52,000.	54,000.	2,883	2,927	2,793	2,797	2,791	2,785	2,779	2,773	2,767
54,000.	56,000.	3,004	3,048	2,915	2,938	2,934	2,928	2,922	2,916	2,911
56,000.	58,000.	3,125	3,169	3,036	3,060	3,077	3,071	3,065	3,060	3,054
58,000.	60,000.	3,247	3,290	3,157	3,181	3,205	3,218	3,214	3,210	3,207

COMPUTE 8.98 PER CENT ON WAGES IN EXCESS OF MAXIMUM SHOWN ABOVE AND ADD TO LAST TAX AMOUNT IN APPLICABLE COLUMN.

NOTE: The tax rates for individual states are varied, and the method of calculating state income tax also varies from state to state. For this reason, the majority of the exercises in this LIFEPAC will not show state income tax as a deduction on the sample payroll registers and employee earnings records.

Voluntary Payroll Deductions

Employees may elect to have money withheld for various voluntary deductions. All voluntary deductions must be authorized in writing by the employee. This requirement holds true whether the deduction is individually applied or part of a group plan. Deductions such as charity contribution, loan repayments and deposits to savings accounts are made by the individual employee. The group plan deductions include union dues, health and life insurance, and retirement plans.

Employer Payroll Taxes

Federal Unemployment Tax. The Federal Unemployment Tax (FUTA) is a federal tax used for administration of state and federal unemployment programs. The two purposes of this tax are: (1) to help states create a state unemployment system, and (2) to provide funds to states to administer their programs. These provisions help the federal government retain some control over the state programs.

The FUTA tax rate is 0.8% on the first $7,000.00 earned by an employee. The employer must pay this tax. It cannot be deducted from the employees' wages. The report must be filed annually.

State Unemployment Tax. This is a tax imposed by a state to pay benefits to the unemployed. All states maintain their unemployment programs by imposing this tax on the employer. Since the standards for unemployment compensation law are set by the Social Security Act, a certain amount of uniformity exists between states.

The state unemployment tax rate varies throughout the nation. In addition, many states offer an employer merit rating which reduces the tax rate for that business. However, the average imposed tax is 5.4% on the first $7,000.00 earned by an employee. The state unemployment tax must be paid **quarterly**.

Disability Insurance. In addition to Social Security's provision for disability, many states require the employer carry an additional disability policy. This policy covers a percentage of the employee's wages if the employee is injured off the job and is unable to work.

The insurance premiums can be paid by both the employer and the employee. The maximum premium an employee has to pay is $0.60 per week in most states. The balance of the premium is the employer's responsibility. Again, each state has it own regulations related to disability insurance.

Review the material in this section in preparation for the Self Test. The Self Test will check your mastery of this particular section. The items missed on this Self Test will indicate specific areas where restudy is needed for mastery.

SELF TEST 1

Complete the following activities (each answer, 5 points).

1.01 List the major requirements for payroll accounting.

    a. WITHHOLDINGS FROM employee's wages

    b. employer payroll Taxes

    c. employees benefit PROGRAMS maintained by the employeer

1.02 List the three major payroll functions performed by a business.

    a. HIRING

    b. Timekeeping

    c. preparing & paying payroll

1.03 What three payroll deductions are required by law?

    a. Social Security Taxes

    b. Federal Income Taxes

    c. State Income Taxes

1.04 Which form is used to indicate the number of withholding allowances? W-4

1.05 What are the two items listed on the above-mentioned form that are used to determine the amount of federal income tax to be withheld?

    a. MARITAL STATUS

    b. NUMBER of allowences or dependents

1.06 What is the maximum tax base for reporting FICA tax? $76,200

1.07 List four benefits that qualified individuals can receive from the Social Security Administration.

    a. RETIREMENT benefits →   b. disability

    c. Survivor   d. medicare

1.08 What is the maximum tax base for federal and state unemployment taxes?

    $7,000

1.09 Deductions an employee directs an employer to withhold from his/her wages are called

    Voluntary Deductions .

1.010 Who is liable to pay Social Security and Medicare taxes?

    The Employeer & The Employee are BOTH responsible For paying ~~For~~ Social Security & Medicare Taxes.

80 / 100

Score _____

Adult Check _____

Initial   Date

10

SECTION II. CALCULATING EMPLOYEE EARNINGS

Types of Employee Compensation

Salaried. The salary paid to managers, supervisors and other professional employees is a guaranteed annual amount. The salaried employee receives the same pay regardless of total hours worked during a pay period. The reported gross earnings are the same as the stated salary per pay period; therefore, no calculations are needed. As an example, a yearly salary of $32,500 applied to a semimonthly pay period results in a gross pay of $1,250.00 for each pay period. The semimonthly figure of $1,250.00 remains the same regardless of extra time worked at the office or at home. It also remains the same for reasonable time lost from work due to illness.

Hourly. Hourly employees' gross earnings are calculated based on the number of hours worked during the pay period. These employees are paid on an hourly basis for a 40-hour week. By federal regulation, any hours in excess of 40 are considered overtime.

The overtime rate is one and one-half times the regular pay rate. This is referred to as **time and a half**. Some companies vary the overtime rate, but it can never result in a figure less than one and one-half times the employee's regular rate of pay.

Most hourly employees are also covered by the federal minimum wage law. Under this federal regulation the minimum hourly rate, as of this writing, is $5.15 for most occupations. Certain occupations require a lesser minimum wage; therefore, it is important to check the minimum wage by occupation in the Fair Labor Standards booklet. It is also true that because of competition, the minimum hourly rate offered may be higher than the federal law mandates.

Calculate the gross pay for these hourly employees.

2.1   Multiply the hours worked times the hourly rate to calculate the gross earnings for these employees.

Employee	Hours Worked	Hourly Rate	Gross Pay
Karl Kern	34	$12.00	a. $408
John Green	40	$6.75	b. $270
Jack Rowe	38	$11.00	c. $418
Sally Johnson	39	$16.00	d. $624

 Calculate the overtime rate for these hourly rates.

2.2   Multiply the regular rate by 1.5 (time and a half) to find the overtime rate. (NOTE: *Do not* round up the overtime rate until it is applied to overtime hours). The first one is done for you as an example.

Hourly Rate	X Overtime Factor (1.5)	= Overtime Hourly Rate
$9.25	$9.25 x 1.5	$13.875
$12.00	a. $12.00 x 1.5	$18.00
$6.75	b. $6.75 x 1.5	$10.125
$11.00	c. $11.00 x 1.5	$16.50
$16.00	d. $16.00 x 1.5	$24.00

 Calculate the overtime hours.

2.3   The company's pay period is based on a 40-hour week. To find weekly overtime hours, subtract the total hours worked from the required 40-hour week.

a. 42 hours worked   =   _____2_____ hours of overtime

b. 48 hours worked   =   _____8_____ hours of overtime

c. 53 hours worked   =   _____13_____ hours of overtime

d. 34 hours worked   =   _____0_____ hours of overtime

e. 46 hours worked   =   _____6_____ hours of overtime

12

Another method of determining overtime is to include any hours worked over the regular 8-hour day (as opposed to the 40-hour week). By using this method, an employee is paid overtime on a daily basis if he/she works more than 8 hours on a given day. The overtime rate is still one and one-half times the regular rate.

Example:	Hours Worked	Regular Hours	Overtime Hours
Monday	9.0	8	1
Tuesday	6.0	6	0
Wednesday	10.0	8	2
Thursday	8.0	8	0
Friday	10.5	_8_	_2.5_
Total		**38**	**5.5**

 Calculate the the regular and overtime hours for an 8-hour day.

2.4

Employee #1		Regular & Overtime Hours	
Weekdays	**Hours Worked**	**Regular Hours**	**Overtime Hours**
Monday	10	a. 8	2
Tuesday	6	b. 6	0
Wednesday	9	c. 8	1
Thursday	7	d. 7	0
Friday	11	e. 8	3
TOTALS		f. 37	6

Employee #2		Regular & Overtime Hours	
Weekdays	**Hours Worked**	**Regular Hours**	**Overtime Hours**
Monday	9	g. 8	1
Tuesday	8	h. 8	0
Wednesday	10	i. 8	2
Thursday	5	j. 5	0
Friday	12	k. 8	4
TOTALS		l. 37	7

Piecework Employees (Unit of Production).

Many industries, in order to encourage increased production, pay employees on a piece rate basis. The employee is paid a specified amount for each unit produced. Each unit is referred to as a *piece,* and the pay rate is called the *piece rate*.

To find the total earnings, multiply the total number of pieces by the piece rate.

Units Produced	Piece Rate	Gross Pay
310	$1.05	$325.50
1,280	$.35	$448.00

 Calculate gross pay using the unit of production method.

2.5

Employee	Units Produced	Piece Rate	Gross Pay
Lacy Schultz	210	$0.75	a. $157.50
Mary Moore	189	$2.40	b. $453.60
Manuel Smith	110	$1.858	c. $204.38
Margaret Zee	275	$1.15	d. $316.25
Michael Jones	328	$0.97	e. $318.16
Jerry Jenson	299	$1.00	f. $299

STOP

Employee Time Cards

The time card is the best way for most businesses to keep an accurate record of the hours worked by employees. The time card records (1) the time of the employee's arrival, (2) the time the employee leaves work, and (3) the total hours worked each day. The method of recording information on the time card may be completed manually or by an automatic time clock.

In order to manage labor costs, companies have supervisors or managers verify the accuracy of the employees' time cards. This procedure also applies to overtime hours. These hours must be approved by each employee's supervisor.

Quarter Hour Timekeeping. Unfortunately, no matter how the time card is prepared, employees very seldom arrive or depart exactly at a stated hour. To solve the arrival and departure time problem, most companies round to the nearest quarter hour. This system permits the company to pay the employee to the nearest quarter hour regardless of the arrival time or departure time. An example of quarter hour timekeeping is illustrated on the next page:

14

QUARTER HOUR TIMEKEEPING			
Clock Time In	Clock Time Out	Payroll Time In	Payroll Time Out
8:55	12:27	9:00	12:30
9:00	12:01	9:00	12:00
8:48	12:06	9:00	12:00
7:03	11:29	7:00	11:30
8:45	12:05	8:45	12:00

Complete the following activity.

2.6   Use the quarter hour timekeeping method to calculate the correct arrival and departure times.

Clock Time In	Clock Time Out	Payroll Time In	Payroll Time Out
7:55	12:07	a. 8:00	12:00
11:58	1:01	b. 12:00	1:00
8:57	1:06	c. 9:00	1:00
8:03	12:29	d. 8:00	12:30
7:45	11:05	e. 7:45	11:00

Analyzing a Time Card. Shown below is a time card for an employee of the ABC Company. The ABC Company requires its employees to work 8 hours a day. The starting time is 8:00 a.m. Departure time is 5:00 p.m. Lunch is from 12:00 noon to 1:00 p.m. The company calculates time to the nearest quarter hour and pays overtime for any hours worked over a regular 8-hour day.

Employee	David W. Salt		ABC
Employee #	16		
Period Ending	December 31, 20—		Company

DATE	MORNING		AFTERNOON		OVERTIME		HOURS	
	IN	OUT	IN	OUT	IN	OUT	REG	OT
12/27	7:57	12:00	12:57	5:06			8.0	0
12/28	7:59	12:01	12:55	5:01			8.0	0
12/29	8:00	12:00	12:59	5:00	6:03	8:29	8.0	2.5
12/30	7:56	11:58	1:01	5:05			8.0	0
12/31	7:55	12:03	12:58	5:02			8.0	0

	HOURS	RATE	AMOUNT
REGULAR	40.0	8.50	340.00
OVERTIME	2.5	12.75	31.88
TOTAL HOURS	42.5	TOTAL EARNINGS	371.88

Supervisor's OT Approval _____ Joe Jensen _____

Employee's Signature _____ David W. Salt _____

Complete the following activity.

2.7 Shown below is a time card for another employee of the ABC Company. Carefully review the time card on the previous page, and use it as an example to complete this activity.

a. Calculate and **enter directly on the time card** the total regular hours worked each day, rounding to the nearest the quarter hour.

b. Calculate any overtime hours, keeping in mind that the company pays time and a half for any hours worked over the regular 8-hour day.

c. Enter the regular hours worked at the bottom of the card and calculate gross regular wages using the employee's hourly rate.

d. Enter the overtime hours worked, figure and enter the overtime rate (time and a half) and then calculate the overtime wages.

e. Refer to the previous example to complete the time card, calculating total hours and total earnings.

Employee ___*Sue Wetzel*___

Employee # ___*13*___

Period Ending ___*December 31, 20—*___

ABC Company

DATE	MORNING		AFTERNOON		OVERTIME		HOURS	
	IN	OUT	IN	OUT	IN	OUT	REG	OT
12/27	7:59	12:02	12:55	5:06			8.0	0
12/28	8:01	12:00	12:55	5:01	6:03	8:57	8.0	3.0
12/29	8:00	12:00	12:59	5:00			8.0	0
12/30	7:56	11:58	1:01	5:04			8.0	0
12/31	7:55	12:03	12:58	5:02	6:30	9:06	8.0	2.5

	HOURS	RATE	AMOUNT
REGULAR	40.0	9.00	360
OVERTIME	5.5	13.50	74.25
TOTAL HOURS	45.5	TOTAL EARNINGS	434.25

Supervisor's OT Approval ___*Joe Jensen*___

Employee's Signature ___Sue Wetzel___

17

Review the material in this section in preparation for the Self Test. This Self Test will check your mastery of this particular section as well as your knowledge of the previous section.

SELF TEST 2

Match the following accounting terms with their definitions (each answer, 2 points).

2.01 ___j___ period covered by a salary or wage payment

2.02 ___D___ the number of persons legally supported by the taxpayer

2.03 ___K___ Social Security and Medicare taxes

2.04 ___l___ required and voluntary deductions from gross earnings to determine net pay

2.05 ___e___ amount due an employee before deductions

2.06 ___a___ payment based on a fixed monthly or annual rate

2.07 ___G___ tax used to administer federal and state unemployment programs

2.08 ___b___ all salaries and wages paid to employees

2.09 ___C___ payment based on an hourly rate or on a piecework basis

2.010 ___i___ a state tax imposed to pay benefits to the unemployed

2.011 ___F___ the rate a worker is paid for overtime

a. salary

b. payroll

c. wages

d. withholding allowance

e. gross earnings

f. time and a half

g. FUTA

h. net earnings

i. state unemployment tax

j. payroll period

k. FICA

l. payroll deductions

On the blank, print a _T_ if the statement is true or an _F_ if the statement is false (each answer, 2 points).

2.012 ___T___ The first responsibility of the Social Security Act was to assign a Social Security number to each employee in the United States.

2.013 ___F___ It is the normal practice of most companies to allow hourly employees to work as much overtime as they want without supervisor approval.

2.014 ___T___ Group insurance and retirement plans are examples of voluntary payroll deductions.

2.015 ___F___ The Social Security Act was enacted in 19ᶾ5 by President Franklin D. Roosevelt.

2.016 ___T___ Form W-4 is the form that lists an employee's marital status and withholding allowances.

2.017 ___T___ The employer must contribute to Social Security programs at the same rate as the employee.

2.018 ___F___ The salary paid to managers, supervisors and other professional employees is an hourly rate.

ACCOUNTING

eight

LIFEPAC TEST

Name _____

Date _____

Score _____

LIFEPAC TEST ACCOUNTING 8

93%

PART I

On the blank, print a _T_ if the statement is true or an _F_ if the statement is false (each answer, 1 point).

1. **T** Most businesses find that employee payroll and related payroll taxes comprise a large portion of their annual expenses.

2. **T** It is the employer's responsibility to withhold certain payroll taxes from his employees' wages each pay period.

3. **T** An employer is required by federal law to provide an employee benefit program.

4. **T** Both federal and state governments regulate the payroll records that an employer is required to keep.

5. **T** The advantage of a time clock system is that a time clock records the employee's arrival and departure time electronically.

6. **T** An employee earnings record is completed from the information recorded on the employee's time card.

7. **T** Federal income tax and FICA tax are two required deductions from an employee's total earnings.

8. **F** The business form used to summarize payroll transactions is the general journal.

9. **T** The United States Congress has removed limits on the taxable income base for Medicare tax.

10. **T** The amount of federal income tax withheld is determined by the employee's total earnings, marital status and withholding allowances claimed.

11. **T** In addition to retirement benefits, the federal Social Security program also provides survivor's coverage for the employee's spouse and dependents.

12. **T** Employees that are married and supporting dependents usually pay less in income taxes than a single employee.

13. **T** A W-4 form informs the employer of the number of withholding allowances claimed by an employee.

14. **F** Net pay is determined by adding total deductions to total earnings.

15. **F** All payroll taxes are calculated using the employee's net pay.

16. **F** The FICA tax is paid on the total earnings of each employee who has not met the maximum tax base.

17. **F** The federal government provides an exemption from income taxes for salaried employees.

18. **T** The payroll register is used to record all payroll deductions.

19. **F** The tax rate for Social Security and Medicare taxes increases as the employee's total earnings increase.

1

For each statement below, circle the letter of the choice that best completes the sentence (each answer, 1 point).

20.   Total earnings are calculated by applying this formula:
   a. total hours worked times total hourly rate
   b. total regular hours times regular rate, plus overtime hours times overtime rate times 1.5
   c. total regular hours times regular rate, plus overtime hours times overtime rate

21.   A W-4 form contains the following information:
   a. marital status and wage rate
   b. Social Security number, marital status, and number of allowances claimed
   c. place of employment, employee's job title, and marital status

22.   To determine an employee's federal income tax withholding, the employer must know:
   a. total earnings, payroll period, marital status, and number of allowances claimed
   b. marital status, wages, and number of allowances claimed
   c. total earnings, marital status, and number of allowances claimed

23.   Which of the following taxes cannot be deducted from an employee's wages?
   a. FICA tax
   b. federal unemployment taxes
   c. federal income taxes

24.   The total amount due to an employee after all payroll deductions is:
   a. total earnings
   b. net pay
   c. overtime pay

25.   When employees are paid by the number of pieces completed and accepted, these employees are paid:
   a. on a piece rate basis
   b. on an hourly rate
   c. on a stated salary

26.   By federal law the maximum hours an employee can work without being paid overtime is:
   a. 48
   b. 35
   c. 40

27.   To calculate the overtime rate, the regular rate is multiplied by:
   a. one and one-half times
   b. two times
   c. one and three-quarters

28.   The accumulated earnings column on an employee earnings record represents total earnings for the:
   a. month
   b. year
   c. pay period

29. A payroll system which allows the payroll clerk to write the same information on several forms at one time is a:
   a. computer system
   b. professional system
   c. pegboard system

Match the following accounting terms with their definitions (each answer, 1 point).

30. __K__ period covered by a salary or wage payment

31. __E__ the number of persons legally supported by the taxpayer

32. __L__ Social Security and Medicare taxes

33. __N__ summarizes payroll payments made to each individual employee.

34. __D__ summarizes payroll information for all employees during a specific pay period

35. __M__ required and voluntary deductions from gross earnings to determine net pay

36. __f.__ amount due an employee before deductions

37. __a__ payment based on a fixed monthly or annual rate

38. __h__ tax used to administer federal and state unemployment programs

39. __b__ all salaries and wages paid to employees

40. __c__ payment based on an hourly rate or on a piece-work basis

41. __j.__ a state tax imposed to pay benefits to the unemployed

42. __G.__ the rate a worker is paid for overtime

a. salary

b. payroll

c. wages

d. payroll register

e. withholding allowance

f. gross earnings

g. time and a half

h. FUTA

i. net earnings

j. state unemployment tax

k. payroll period

l. FICA

m. payroll deductions

n. earnings record

3

MARRIED Persons- WEEKLY Payroll Period

(For Wages Paid in 2000)

If the wages are-		And the number of withholding allowances claimed is-										
At least	But less than	0	1	2	3	4	5	6	7	8	9	10
		The amount of income tax to be withheld is-										
$0	$125	0	0	0	0	0	0	0	0	0	0	0
125	130	1	0	0	0	0	0	0	0	0	0	0
130	135	1	0	0	0	0	0	0	0	0	0	0
135	140	2	0	0	0	0	0	0	0	0	0	0
140	145	3	0	0	0	0	0	0	0	0	0	0
145	150	4	0	0	0	0	0	0	0	0	0	0
150	155	4	0	0	0	0	0	0	0	0	0	0
155	160	5	0	0	0	0	0	0	0	0	0	0
160	165	6	0	0	0	0	0	0	0	0	0	0
165	170	7	0	0	0	0	0	0	0	0	0	0
170	175	7	0	0	0	0	0	0	0	0	0	0
175	180	8	0	0	0	0	0	0	0	0	0	0
180	185	9	1	0	0	0	0	0	0	0	0	0
185	190	10	1	0	0	0	0	0	0	0	0	0
190	195	10	2	0	0	0	0	0	0	0	0	0
195	200	11	3	0	0	0	0	0	0	0	0	0
200	210	12	4	0	0	0	0	0	0	0	0	0
210	220	14	6	0	0	0	0	0	0	0	0	0
220	230	15	7	0	0	0	0	0	0	0	0	0
230	240	17	9	0	0	0	0	0	0	0	0	0
240	250	18	10	2	0	0	0	0	0	0	0	0
250	260	20	12	3	0	0	0	0	0	0	0	0
260	270	21	13	5	0	0	0	0	0	0	0	0
270	280	23	15	6	0	0	0	0	0	0	0	0
280	290	24	16	8	0	0	0	0	0	0	0	0
290	300	26	18	9	1	0	0	0	0	0	0	0
300	310	27	19	11	3	0	0	0	0	0	0	0
310	320	29	21	12	4	0	0	0	0	0	0	0
320	330	30	22	14	6	0	0	0	0	0	0	0
330	340	32	24	15	7	0	0	0	0	0	0	0
340	350	33	25	17	9	1	0	0	0	0	0	0
350	360	35	27	18	10	2	0	0	0	0	0	0
360	370	36	28	20	12	4	0	0	0	0	0	0
370	380	38	30	21	13	5	0	0	0	0	0	0
380	390	39	31	23	15	7	0	0	0	0	0	0
390	400	41	33	24	16	8	0	0	0	0	0	0
400	410	42	34	26	18	10	2	0	0	0	0	0
410	420	44	36	27	19	11	3	0	0	0	0	0
420	430	45	37	29	21	13	5	0	0	0	0	0
430	440	47	39	30	22	14	6	0	0	0	0	0
440	450	48	40	32	24	16	8	0	0	0	0	0
450	460	50	42	33	25	17	9	1	0	0	0	0
460	470	51	43	35	27	19	11	3	0	0	0	0
470	480	53	45	36	28	20	12	4	0	0	0	0
480	490	54	46	38	30	22	14	6	0	0	0	0
490	500	56	48	39	31	23	15	7	0	0	0	0
500	510	57	49	41	33	25	17	9	1	0	0	0
510	520	59	51	42	34	26	18	10	2	0	0	0
520	530	60	52	44	36	28	20	12	4	0	0	0
530	540	62	54	45	37	29	21	13	5	0	0	0
540	550	63	55	47	39	31	23	15	7	0	0	0
550	560	65	57	48	40	32	24	16	8	0	0	0
560	570	66	58	50	42	34	26	18	10	2	0	0
570	580	68	60	51	43	35	27	19	11	3	0	0
580	590	69	61	53	45	37	29	21	13	5	0	0
590	600	71	63	54	46	38	30	22	14	6	0	0
600	610	72	64	56	48	40	32	24	16	8	0	0
610	620	74	66	57	49	41	33	25	17	9	1	0
620	630	75	67	59	51	43	35	27	19	11	2	0
630	640	77	69	60	52	44	36	28	20	12	4	0
640	650	78	70	62	54	46	38	30	22	14	5	0
650	660	80	72	63	55	47	39	31	23	15	7	0
660	670	81	73	65	57	49	41	33	25	17	8	0
670	680	83	75	66	58	50	42	34	26	18	10	2
680	690	84	76	68	60	52	44	36	28	20	11	3
690	700	86	78	69	61	53	45	37	29	21	13	5
700	710	87	79	71	63	55	47	39	31	23	14	6
710	720	89	81	72	64	56	48	40	32	24	16	8
720	730	90	82	74	66	58	50	42	34	26	17	9
730	740	92	84	75	67	59	51	43	35	27	19	11

PART II

Complete the following activities (49 points total).

Fun-Time Novelties is a small company with only eight employees. Instead of using time cards and a time clock, the company utilizes a time sheet (shown below) to keep track of employee hours worked during a payroll period.

43.   **Complete the time sheet** for the weekly payroll period ended June 25 of the current year.

- Determine regular hours and overtime hours worked. NOTE: The company pays overtime for any hours *in excess 40 hours per week*.
- Calculate regular pay, overtime rate and overtime pay. The first one has been done for you as an example.
- Total the *Regular Earnings* and *Overtime Earnings* columns.

44.   **Complete the payroll register.**

- Transfer regular pay and overtime pay from the time sheet to the payroll register.
- Compute federal withholding tax using the tax table on page 4 of this LIFEPAC Test.
- The company deducts a combined amount for FICA taxes (Social Security and Medicare), so use the correct percentage of total earnings to calculate this deduction for each employee.
- Prove the payroll register by totaling all columns and cross-checking your work (subtract total deductions from total earnings).

Do Not round-up

FUN-TIME NOVELTIES
Time Sheet for the Week Ended *June 25, 20—*

EMPLOYEE NAME	MON	TUES	WED	THURS	FRI	REGULAR HOURS	OVERTIME HOURS	REGULAR RATE	REGULAR EARNINGS	OVERTIME RATE	OVERTIME EARNINGS
Allen, Joseph	9	6	8.5	7	8	38.5	0	8.56	329.56		
Baxter, Tina	8	9.5	7	6	10	40	.5	9.15	366.00	13.725	6.87
Charles, Henry	10	8	7	9	8	40	2	9.35	374.00	14.03	28.06
Day, Nora	7	9	9	10	7	40	2	8.85	354.00	13.28	26.56
Fry, Thomas	8	8	9	10	6	40	1	7.95	318.00	11.93	11.93
George, Marcia	7	9.5	10	6	9	40	1.5	8.10	324.00	12.15	18.23
Howe, Greg	8	6	9	10	7	40	0	7.89	315.60	11.84	0
Jones, Melvin	10	8	9	7	7	40	1	9.25	370.00	13.88	13.88
								Totals	2751.16		105.50

5

PAYROLL REGISTER for the Weekly Payroll Period Ended June 25, 2003

NO.	NAME	MARITAL STATUS	EXEMP.	REGULAR		OVERTIME		TOTAL		FEDERAL INCOME TAX		FICA		HEALTH INSURANCE	OTHER	TOTAL DEDUCTIONS		AMOUNT	
1	Allen, Joseph	M	2	329	56			329	56	12	00	25	21			37	21	292	35
2	Baxton, Tina	M	3	366	00	6	87	372	87	13	00	28	52			41	52	331	35
3	Charles, Henry	M	1	374	00	28	86	402	86	34	00	30	76			64	76	337	30
4	Day, Nora	M	4	354	00	26	56	380	56	7	00	29	11			36	11	344	45
5	Fry, Thomas	M	2	318	00	11	93	329	93	14	00	25	24			39	24	290	69
6	George, Marcia	M	3	324	00	18	23	342	23	9	00	26	18			35	18	307	05
7	Howe, Greg	M	1	315	60			315	60	21	00	24	14			45	14	270	46
8	Jones, Melvin	M	2	370	00	13	88	383	88	23	00	29	37			52	37	331	51
	Totals			2751	16	105	53	2856	69	133	00	218	54			351	53	2505	16

Header groupings: EMPLOYEE DATA (NAME, MARITAL STATUS, EXEMP.); EARNINGS (REGULAR, OVERTIME, TOTAL); DEDUCTIONS (FEDERAL INCOME TAX, FICA, HEALTH INSURANCE, OTHER, TOTAL DEDUCTIONS); NET PAY (AMOUNT)

Margin notes:
6.2
1.45 – medicare
2505.16
7.65
2573.48

6

NOTES

2.019 ___F___ The employee is responsible for his own federal and state unemployment taxes.

2.020 Complete the time card (each answer, 4 points).

a. Calculate and **enter directly on the time card** the total regular hours worked each day, rounding to the nearest the quarter hour.

b. Calculate any overtime hours, keeping in mind that the company pays time and a half for any hours worked over the regular 8-hour day.

c. Enter the regular hours worked at the bottom of the card and calculate gross regular wages using the employee's hourly rate.

d. Enter the overtime hours worked, figure and enter the overtime rate, then calculate the overtime wages.

e. Calculate total hours and total earnings.

Employee ___Katherine Ludwig___

Employee # ___22___

Period Ending ___October 30, 20—___

ABC Company

DATE	MORNING		AFTERNOON		OVERTIME		HOURS	
	IN	OUT	IN	OUT	IN	OUT	REG	OT
10/26	7:55	12:04	1:05	5:03			8.0	0
10/27	8:01	12:00	12:55	5:01	5:33	9:00	8.0	3.5
10/28	8:00	11:59	12:59	5:00			8.0	0
10/29	7:56	11:58	1:01	5:03			8.0	0
10/30	7:55	12:03	12:58	5:02	6:00	8:30	8.0	2.5

	HOURS	RATE	AMOUNT
REGULAR	40.0	8.75	350.00
OVERTIME	6.0	13.13	78.78
TOTAL HOURS	46.0	TOTAL EARNINGS	428.75

Supervisor's OT Approval ___Joe Jensen___

Employee's Signature ___Katherine Ludwig___

85 / 106

Score _____

Ⓥ Adult Check _____

Initial   Date

SECTION III. PAYROLL RECORDS & METHODS

The Payroll Register

By law, each employer is required to keep records of all salaries and wages paid to employees for a period of at least four years. These records must provide several types of payroll data including: (1) the amount of wages or salaries paid; (2) the amounts deducted from the employees' earnings; (3) the expenses involved with the payroll; and (4) the payroll taxes paid by the employer and the employees to the government.

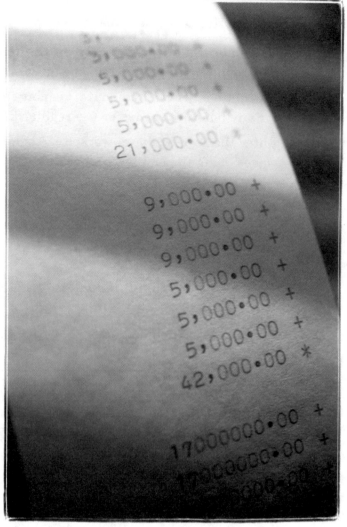

The **payroll register** (illustrated on the next page) is an accounting form that summarizes payroll information for the employees of a business. It itemizes the total earnings and payroll deductions of all employees. The payroll clerk is usually required to complete the register which contains the following information:

1. Each employee's name and employee number;

2. Marital status and withholding allowances (from employee W-4 forms);

3. Regular earnings, overtime earnings and gross earnings (from employee time cards);

4. Federal income tax (from the appropriate tax table), Social Security tax (6.2% of total earnings) and Medicare tax (1.45% of total earnings) withheld;

5. Other deductions, including group health insurance premiums, union dues, etc.;

6. The total deductions—mandatory and voluntary;

7. Net pay after all deductions have been made;

8. The check number for each paycheck written; and

9. When the payroll information for the employees has been recorded in the payroll register, the columns are totaled as shown. The accuracy of the register is proved at this point, before the payroll is paid. The total of the Earnings columns less the total of the Deductions columns should equal the total of the Net Pay column.

Once the accuracy of the payroll register has been verified, the information is recorded in the firm's accounting records. The column totals from the payroll register supply all the necessary figures. Each item in the entry may be traced back to the payroll register.

NOTE: This payroll register is for illustration purposes only. State income tax deductions are not included.

PAYROLL REGISTER for the Semimonthly Payroll Period Ended   March 15, 20—

NO.	EMPLOYEE DATA 1 NAME	2 MARITAL STATUS	EXEMP.	3 EARNINGS REGULAR	OVERTIME	TOTAL	4 DEDUCTIONS FEDERAL INCOME TAX	SOCIAL SECURITY	MEDICARE	5 OTHER	6 TOTAL DEDUCTIONS	7 NET PAY AMOUNT	8 CHECK NO.
3	Bates, Mary	M	3	700 00		700 00	14 00	43 40	10 15	45 00	112 55	587 45	118
1	Clark, Chris	S	1	100 00		100 00	0 00	6 20	1 45		7 65	92 35	119
2	Jones, Harry	M	3	700 00	50 00	750 00	20 00	46 50	10 88	45 00	122 38	627 62	120
4	Jones, Mildred	S	1	800 00		800 00	87 00	49 60	11 60		148 20	651 80	121
9	King, Mary	S	1	800 00		800 00	87 00	49 60	11 60		148 20	651 80	122
6	Lowe, Howard	M	2	250 00		250 00	0 00	15 50	3 63		19 13	230 87	123
8	Martin, John	M	1	695 00		695 00	46 00	43 09	10 08		99 17	595 83	124
7	Ness, Elton	S	0	185 00		185 00	12 00	11 47	2 68		26 15	158 85	125
5	Zybrinski, Carol	S	1	600 00	22 50	622 50	60 00	38 60	9 03	20 00	127 63	494 87	126
9	Totals			4830 00	72 50	4902 50	326 00	303 96	71 10	110 00	811 06	4091 44	

21

The Employee Earnings Record

The **employee earnings record** is the form used to reflect the payroll payments made to each employee. The information must be entered on the earnings record every pay period. The individual employee earnings record shows total earnings, payroll deductions, net pay, and accumulated earnings for the entire year. This form is used by the payroll clerk to complete the required tax forms at the end of the year.

Normally, a record card is kept for each employee. The amount columns on an individual earnings record are the same as those on a payroll register. However, one additional column is added to the earnings record. This column is called "Accumulated Earnings." The purpose of this column is to keep a running total of each employee's gross earnings; therefore, at any given time the payroll clerk can find total accumulated earnings for each employee from the beginning of the calendar year to its end.

Individual earnings records are kept on a quarterly basis. This makes it easier for businesses to complete government reports that are filed each quarter. At the end of each quarter, the amount columns are totaled. The final amount in the accumulated earnings column is carried forward to use as a beginning figure for the next quarter.

EMPLOYEE EARNINGS RECORD
for the Quarter Ended _March 31, 20—_

Bates, Mary **1**
1910 Marywood Ave.
Binghamton, NY 13905

EMPLOYEE NO.:	3	MARITAL STATUS:	m
POSITION:	Supervisor	ALLOWANCES:	2
RATE OF PAY:	$1400.⁰⁰/mo.	SSN:	111-06-9870

2 PAY PERIOD		**3** EARNINGS			DEDUCTIONS					ACCUMULATED EARNINGS	
PAY NO.	ENDED	REGULAR	OVERTIME	TOTAL	FEDERAL INCOME TAX	SOCIAL SECURITY	MEDICARE	OTHER	TOTAL DEDUCTIONS	NET PAY	**4** YEAR TO DATE
1	1-15	700 00		700 00	14 00	43 40	10 15	45 00	112 55	587 45	700 00
2	1-31	700 00		700 00	14 00	43 40	10 15	45 00	112 55	587 45	1400 00
3	2-15	700 00		700 00	14 00	43 40	10 15	45 00	112 55	587 45	2100 00
4	2-29	700 00		700 00	14 00	43 40	10 15	45 00	112 55	587 45	2800 00
5	3-15	700 00		700 00	14 00	43 40	10 15	45 00	112 55	587 45	3500 00
6	**5** 3-31	700 00		700 00	14 00	43 40	10 15	45 00	112 55	587 45	4200 00
	Totals	4200 00		4200 00	84 00	260 40	60 90	270 00	675 30	3524 70	

1. Personal information is obtained from the employment application and the employee's W-4 form. If the company has a human resources department, that department sends the information on new hires to the payroll department with instructions to place the individual on the payroll.

2. The pay period information lists the pay week number for the quarter and the ending date of that pay period.

3. The earnings, deductions and net pay amounts come from the payroll register and are entered after each payroll period.

4. The year-to-date amount in the accumulated earnings column is calculated by adding the *total earnings* from January 15th to the total earnings from January 31st, and so on. Total earnings, rather than net pay, are recorded in this column because when filing payroll tax reports, the employer must report not only the payroll taxes withheld but also the gross earnings from which those payroll taxes were deducted.

5. At the end of each quarter all of the amount columns are totaled. (NOTE: Since the accumulated earnings amount is a running total, it is not totaled.) The accuracy of these totals is verified by subtracting total deductions from total earnings.

Other Payroll Methods

The Pegboard System. The design of this manual payroll system allows the payroll clerk to enter the same information at one time on several forms. The pegboard system consists of a rigid board with a row of evenly-spaced pegs down its side. The forms have a punched strip on the side with evenly-spaced holes that correspond to the pegs on the pegboard. Each form has a carbon strip on the back, and when the forms are placed on the pegboard in the correct order and  at the proper location on the pegs, a single entry can complete the payroll register, the employee earnings record and the payroll check.

The major advantage of this system is that the information is transferred to several forms at once, thus saving time and reducing errors.

Computerized Systems. Payroll software packages provide an organized system of preparing, storing and retrieving payroll records. The software saves time by calculating total earnings, searching the tax tables, completing employee earnings records and preparing payroll checks. The computer also does all the of calculations related to required and voluntary deductions and net pay.

The computer program with its storage files can keep all payroll records together in one place. These files are easily stored and information can be easily and quickly retrieved as needed. Using a computerized payroll system provides additional accuracy and reduces the time spent in payroll preparation.

Professional Payroll Services. These are private companies that provide payroll services for many businesses. The service collects payroll data, prepares all registers and reports and maintains the payroll records. By using a professional service, a business can save time and payroll costs. Since a service of this type is provided outside of the firm, there are additional costs involved with its use.

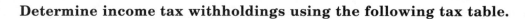

Determine income tax withholdings using the following tax table.

3.1

MARRIED Persons- **WEEKLY** Payroll Period

(For Wages Paid in 2000)

If the wages are-		And the number of withholding allowances claimed is-										
At least	But less than	0	1	2	3	4	5	6	7	8	9	10
		The amount of income tax to be withheld is-										
$0	$125	0	0	0	0	0	0	0	0	0	0	0
125	130	1	0	0	0	0	0	0	0	0	0	0
130	135	1	0	0	0	0	0	0	0	0	0	0
135	140	2	0	0	0	0	0	0	0	0	0	0
140	145	3	0	0	0	0	0	0	0	0	0	0
145	150	4	0	0	0	0	0	0	0	0	0	0
150	155	4	0	0	0	0	0	0	0	0	0	0
155	160	5	0	0	0	0	0	0	0	0	0	0
160	165	6	0	0	0	0	0	0	0	0	0	0
165	170	7	0	0	0	0	0	0	0	0	0	0
170	175	7	0	0	0	0	0	0	0	0	0	0
175	180	8	0	0	0	0	0	0	0	0	0	0
180	185	9	1	0	0	0	0	0	0	0	0	0
185	190	10	1	0	0	0	0	0	0	0	0	0
190	195	10	2	0	0	0	0	0	0	0	0	0
195	200	11	3	0	0	0	0	0	0	0	0	0
200	210	12	4	0	0	0	0	0	0	0	0	0
210	220	14	6	0	0	0	0	0	0	0	0	0
220	230	15	7	0	0	0	0	0	0	0	0	0
230	240	17	9	0	0	0	0	0	0	0	0	0
240	250	18	10	2	0	0	0	0	0	0	0	0
250	260	20	12	3	0	0	0	0	0	0	0	0
260	270	21	13	5	0	0	0	0	0	0	0	0
270	280	23	15	6	0	0	0	0	0	0	0	0
280	290	24	16	8	0	0	0	0	0	0	0	0
290	300	26	18	9	1	0	0	0	0	0	0	0
300	310	27	19	11	3	0	0	0	0	0	0	0
310	320	29	21	12	4	0	0	0	0	0	0	0
320	330	30	22	14	6	0	0	0	0	0	0	0
330	340	32	24	15	7	0	0	0	0	0	0	0
340	350	33	25	17	9	1	0	0	0	0	0	0
350	360	35	27	18	10	2	0	0	0	0	0	0
360	370	36	28	20	12	4	0	0	0	0	0	0
370	380	38	30	21	13	5	0	0	0	0	0	0
380	390	39	31	23	15	7	0	0	0	0	0	0
390	400	41	33	24	16	8	0	0	0	0	0	0
400	410	42	34	26	18	10	2	0	0	0	0	0
410	420	44	36	27	19	11	3	0	0	0	0	0
420	430	45	37	29	21	13	5	0	0	0	0	0
430	440	47	39	30	22	14	6	0	0	0	0	0
440	450	48	40	32	24	16	8	0	0	0	0	0
450	460	50	42	33	25	17	9	1	0	0	0	0
460	470	51	43	35	27	19	11	3	0	0	0	0
470	480	53	45	36	28	20	12	4	0	0	0	0
480	490	54	46	38	30	22	14	6	0	0	0	0
490	500	56	48	39	31	23	15	7	0	0	0	0
500	510	57	49	41	33	25	17	9	1	0	0	0
510	520	59	51	42	34	26	18	10	2	0	0	0
520	530	60	52	44	36	28	20	12	4	0	0	0
530	540	62	54	45	37	29	21	13	5	0	0	0
540	550	63	55	47	39	31	23	15	7	0	0	0
550	560	65	57	48	40	32	24	16	8	0	0	0
560	570	66	58	50	42	34	26	18	10	2	0	0
570	580	68	60	51	43	35	27	19	11	3	0	0
580	590	69	61	53	45	37	29	21	13	5	0	0
590	600	71	63	54	46	38	30	22	14	6	0	0
600	610	72	64	56	48	40	32	24	16	8	0	0
610	620	74	66	57	49	41	33	25	17	9	1	0
620	630	75	67	59	51	43	35	27	19	11	2	0
630	640	77	69	60	52	44	36	28	20	12	4	0
640	650	78	70	62	54	46	38	30	22	14	5	0
650	660	80	72	63	55	47	39	31	23	15	7	0
660	670	81	73	65	57	49	41	33	25	17	8	0
670	680	83	75	66	58	50	42	34	26	18	10	2
680	690	84	76	68	60	52	44	36	28	20	11	3
690	700	86	78	69	61	53	45	37	29	21	13	5
700	710	87	79	71	63	55	47	39	31	23	14	6
710	720	89	81	72	64	56	48	40	32	24	16	8
720	730	90	82	74	66	58	50	42	34	26	17	9
730	740	92	84	75	67	59	51	43	35	27	19	11

Page 38

Allowances	Total Earnings	Tax Withheld	Allowances	Total Earnings	Tax Withheld
1	$116.00	a. _0_	2	$355.75	h. $18
1	$122.00	b. _0_	1	$540.95	i. $55
0	$130.00	c. $1	6	$648.25	j. $30
0	$125.00	d. $1	5	$585.00	k. $29
1	$100.00	e. _0_	0	$270.00	l. $23
3	$240.00	f. _0_	3	$560.00	m. $42
2	$349.75	g. $17	4	$725.00	n. $58

24

Complete the following activity.

GOOD! O.K.

a. **Prepare the semimonthly payroll register** below for the payroll period ended March 15th of the current year.

b. **Calculate federal income tax withholding** using the tax tables shown on pages 31–34.

c. **Calculate FICA withholdings.** The company combines Social Security and Medicare, so use the FICA tax rate of 7.65%.

d. **Total the columns** (down and across) to check the accuracy of your work.

PAYROLL REGISTER for the Semimonthly Payroll Period Ended March 15, 2003

NO.	NAME	MARITAL STATUS	EXEMP.	EARNINGS REGULAR	EARNINGS OVERTIME	EARNINGS TOTAL	FEDERAL INCOME TAX	FICA	DEDUCTIONS GROUP HEALTH INSURANCE	DEDUCTIONS OTHER	DEDUCTIONS TOTAL DEDUCTIONS	NET PAY AMOUNT
1	Bentley, James	M	2	806 00		806 00	$ 46 00	$ 61 66			107 66	698 34
5	Clark, Chris	S	1	425 00		425 00	$ 30 00	$ 32 51			62 51	362 49
3	Day, Horace	M	3	751 00	60 00	811 00	$ 29 00	$ 62 04			91 04	719 96
6	Finch, Mike	M	1	570 00		570 00	$ 28 00	$ 43 61			71 61	498 39
2	Green, Jack	S	1	490 00	38 00	528 00	$ 45 00	$ 40 39			85 39	442 61
4	Howard, Mary	S	0	629 60	22 00	651 60	$ 81 00	$ 49 85			130 85	520 75
7	Lowe, Tom	M	1	859 60	22 75	882 35	$ 76 00	$ 67 90			143 90	738 85
12	Moore, Mary	M	3	815 00		815 00	$ 29 00	$ 62 35			91 35	723 65
11	North, Robert	S	1	687 00	32 00	719 00	$ 72 00	$ 55 00			127 00	592 00
10	Paul, Harry	M	3	768 00	11 00	779 00	$ 23 00	$ 59 59			82 59	696 41
8	Smith, Joe	S	0	592 00		592 00	$ 72 00	$ 45 29			117 29	474 71
9	Wilson, Joan	M	2	572 00	19 50	591 50	$ 15 00	$ 45 25			58 25	533 25
	Totals			7965 80	205 25	8170 45	540 00	625 64			1169 04	7001 41

Review the material in this section in preparation for the Self Test. This Self Test will check your mastery of this particular section as well as your knowledge of the previous sections.

3.01 **Calculate gross wages from time cards** (54 points total).

a. Determine regular, overtime and total hours worked by each employee. Any hours over an 8-hour day are considered overtime.

b. Calculate the regular, overtime and total earnings, and complete the time cards below.

Employee No. 6

Name Harrison Ford

Period Ending January 15, 20—

Morning		Afternoon		Overtime		Hours	
IN	OUT	IN	OUT	IN	OUT	REG	OT
7:59	12:01	1:00	5:02			8.0	0
8:03	11:59	1:01	5:03			8.0	0
8:00	12:00	1:02	5:00			8.0	0
7:56	11:57	1:01	5:03	6:00	8:00	8.0	2.0
7:59	12:03	1:00	5:00			8.0	0
							0
8:01	12:00	1:03	5:00			8.0	0
7:56	11:58	1:00	5:04	6:30	7:30	8.0	1.0
8:00	12:00	1:01	5:01			8.0	0
7:58	11:57	1:05	5:06	6:00	8:45	8.0	2.75
7:59	12:04	1:00	5:01			8.0	0

	HOURS	RATE	AMOUNT
REGULAR	80	9.50	760.00
OVERTIME	5.75	14.25	81.94
TOTAL	85.75		841.94

Employee No. 8

Name Mike Black

Period Ending January 15, 20—

Morning		Afternoon		Overtime		Hours	
IN	OUT	IN	OUT	IN	OUT	REG	OT
7:59	12:01	1:00	5:02			8.0	
8:03	11:59	1:01	4:03			7.0	
9:00	12:00	1:02	5:00			7.0	
7:56	11:57	1:01	5:03	6:00	8:00	8.0	2
7:59	12:03	1:00	5:00			8.0	
8:01	12:00	1:03	5:00			8.0	
7:56	11:58	1:00	5:04	5:30	7:30	8.0	2
9:00	12:00	1:01	5:01			7.0	
7:58	11:57	1:05	5:06			8.0	
7:59	12:04	1:00	3:01			6.0	

	HOURS	RATE	AMOUNT
REGULAR	75.0	7.40	562.40
OVERTIME	4.0	11.10	44.40
TOTAL	79.0		606.80

a. **Prepare the semimonthly payroll register** below for the payroll period ended June 15th of the current year.

b. **Calculate federal income tax withholding** using the tax tables shown on pages 31–34.

c. **Calculate state income tax withholding** using the tax tables shown on pages 35–37.

d. **Calculate FICA withholdings.** The company combines Social Security and Medicare, so use the FICA tax rate of 7.65%.

e. **Total the columns.**

PAYROLL REGISTER for the Semimonthly Payroll Period Ended June 15, 2005

NO.	EMPLOYEE DATA NAME	MARITAL STATUS	EXEMP.	EARNINGS REGULAR	OVERTIME	TOTAL	DEDUCTIONS FEDERAL INCOME TAX	FICA	STATE INCOME TAX	HEALTH INSURANCE	TOTAL DEDUCTIONS	NET PAY AMOUNT
1	Abbott, Patricia	M	2	522 00	14 80	536 80	4 00	41 07	13 54	30 00	87 61	449 19
5	Adams, Chris	S	1	582 00	22 80	604 80	57 00	46 27	20 30		123 57	481 23
3	Banks, Wilma	M	3	645 00	28 30	673 30	8 00	51 51	13 18	38 00	110 69	562 61
6	French, Donna	M	2	370 00	0	370 00	0	28 31	5 48	30 00	63 79	306 21
2	Griffith, Mindy	M	4	692 00	38 00	730 00	0	55 85	10 46		66 31	663 69
4	Harris, James	S	0	696 00	32 00	728 00	93 00	55 69	30 74		116 43	551 57
7	Jones, Tom	M	1	680 00		680 00	46 00	52 02	23 66	30 00	151 68	528 32
12	Martin, Mary	M	2	708 00	12 00	720 00	34 00	55 08	20 27	30 00	139 35	580 65
11	Northrop, Greg	S	1	687 00		687 00	99 00	52 56	23 66	28 00	173 22	513 78
10	Patton, Harry	M	3	568 00	11 00	579 00	0	44 30	9 15	44 00	97 45	481 55
8	Trent, Joe	S	1	592 00	0	592 00	54 00	45 29	19 96	28 00	147 25	444 75
9	Watson, Joanne	S	2	472 00	0	472 00	20 00	36 11	9 85	28 00	93 96	378 04
	Totals			7314 00	158 90	7372 90	385 00	564 06	199 25	282 00	1431 50	5941 59

110 / 137

Score _____

Adult Check _____

Initial   Date

27

IV. REVIEW & APPLICATION PROBLEMS

Complete these activities.

4.1   Calculate the amount of regular, overtime (time and a half) and total earnings for each employee listed below.

Employee Number	Regular Hours	Overtime Hours	Regular Rate	Regular Earnings	Overtime Earnings	Total Earnings
1	40	3	$7.50	300	33.75	333.75
2	40	8	8.25	330	99.00	429
3	40	0	6.00	240		240
4	35	0	5.75	201.25		201.25
5	40	6	6.75	270	60.75	330.75
6	29	0	8.50	246.50		246.50
7	40	2.5	9.25	370.40	34.69	405.09
8	32	0	7.00	224.00		224.00
9	40	1.75	7.25	290.00	19.03	309.03
10	39	0	9.45	368.55		368.55
11	40	3.75	8.35	334	46.97	380.97
12	40	1	5.50	220	8.25	228.25
13	40	8.5	5.15	206	65.66	271.66
14	40	10	6.80	272	102.00	374.00
15	40	1.5	6.30	252	14.18	266.18

4.2   You have just been hired by the XYZ Company. On the next page is the W-4 form the payroll department has given you to complete so that they may send your withholding information to the IRS. Read the instructions carefully then use your own name, address and Social Security number to complete the form.

Form W-4 (2000)

Purpose. Complete Form W-4 so your employer can withhold the correct Federal income tax from your pay. Because your tax situation may change, you may want to refigure your withholding each year.

Exemption from withholding. If you are exempt, complete only lines 1, 2, 3, 4, and 7, and sign the form to validate it. Your exemption for 2000 expires February 16, 2001.

Note: *You cannot claim exemption from withholding if (1) your income exceeds $700 and includes more than $250 of unearned income (e.g., interest and dividends) and (2) another person can claim you as a dependent on their tax return.*

Basic instructions. If you are not exempt, complete the **Personal Allowances Worksheet** below. The worksheets on page 2 adjust your withholding allowances based on itemized deductions, adjustments to income, or two-earner/two-job situations. Complete all worksheets that apply. They will help you figure the number of withholding allowances you are entitled to claim. **However, you may claim fewer (or zero) allowances.**

Child tax and higher education credits. For details on adjusting withholding for these and other credits, see **Pub. 919,** How Do I Adjust My Tax Withholding?

Head of household. Generally, you may claim head of household filing status on your tax return only if you are unmarried and pay more than 50% of the costs of keeping up a home for yourself and your dependent(s) or other qualifying individuals. See line E below.

Nonwage income. If you have a large amount of nonwage income, such as interest or dividends, you should consider making estimated tax payments using **Form 1040-ES,** Estimated Tax for Individuals. Otherwise, you may owe additional tax.

Two earners/two jobs. If you have a working spouse or more than one job, figure the total number of allowances you are entitled to claim on all jobs using worksheets from only one Form W-4. Your withholding usually will be most accurate when all allowances are claimed on the Form W-4 prepared for the highest paying job and zero allowances are claimed for the others.

Check your withholding. After your Form W-4 takes effect, use Pub. 919 to see how the dollar amount you are having withheld compares to your projected total tax for 2000. Get Pub. 919 especially if you used the **Two-Earner/Two-Job Worksheet** on page 2 and your earnings exceed $150,000 (Single) or $200,000 (Married).

Recent name change? If your name on line 1 differs from that shown on your social security card, call 1-800-772-1213 for a new social security card.

Personal Allowances Worksheet (Keep for your records.)

A Enter "1" for **yourself** if no one else can claim you as a dependent . . . . **A** ___1___

B Enter "1" if:
- You are single and have only one job; or
- You are married, have only one job, and your spouse does not work; or
- Your wages from a second job or your spouse's wages (or the total of both) are $1,000 or less.

. . **B** ___1___

C Enter "1" for your **spouse.** But, you may choose to enter -0- if you are married and have either a working spouse or more than one job. (Entering -0- may help you avoid having too little tax withheld.) . . . . **C** _____

D Enter number of **dependents** (other than your spouse or yourself) you will claim on your tax return . . . . **D** _____

E Enter "1" if you will file as **head of household** on your tax return (see conditions under **Head of household** above) . **E** _____

F Enter "1" if you have at least $1,500 of **child or dependent care expenses** for which you plan to claim a credit . . **F** _____

G **Child Tax Credit:**
- If your total income will be between $18,000 and $50,000 ($23,000 and $63,000 if married), enter "1" for each eligible child.
- If your total income will be between $50,000 and $80,000 ($63,000 and $115,000 if married), enter "1" if you have two eligible children, enter "2" if you have three or four eligible children, or enter "3" if you have five or more eligible children **G** _____

H Add lines A through G and enter total here. **Note:** *This may be different from the number of exemptions you claim on your tax return.* ▶ **H** ___1___

For accuracy, complete all worksheets that apply.
- If you plan to **itemize or claim adjustments to income** and want to reduce your withholding, see the **Deductions and Adjustments Worksheet** on page 2.
- If you are **single,** have **more than one job** and your combined earnings from all jobs exceed $34,000, OR if you are **married** and have a **working spouse or more than one job** and the combined earnings from all jobs exceed $60,000, see the **Two-Earner/Two-Job Worksheet** on page 2 to avoid having too little tax withheld.
- If **neither** of the above situations applies, **stop here** and enter the number from line H on line 5 of Form W-4 below.

- **Cut here and give Form W-4 to your employer. Keep the top part for your records.** - - - - - - - - - - - - - - -

---

Form **W-4**
Department of the Treasury
Internal Revenue Service

Employee's Withholding Allowance Certificate

▶ **For Privacy Act and Paperwork Reduction Act Notice, see page 2.**

OMB No. 1545-0010

2000

1 Type or print your first name and middle initial	Last name	2 Your social security number
Aubrey E.	Bird	652 646 1860

Home address (number and street or rural route)
730 Jamison Rd

3 ☑ Single ☐ Married ☐ Married, but withhold at higher Single rate.
Note: *If married, but legally separated, or spouse is a nonresident alien, check the Single box.*

City or town, state, and ZIP code
Elma NY 14059

4 If your last name differs from that on your social security card, check here. **You must call 1-800-772-1213 for a new card** . . . ▶ ☐

5 Total number of allowances you are claiming (from line H above **OR** from the applicable worksheet on page 2) | **5** | 1

6 Additional amount, if any, you want withheld from each paycheck . . . . | **6** | $

7 I claim exemption from withholding for 2000, and I certify that I meet **BOTH** of the following conditions for exemption:
- Last year I had a right to a refund of **ALL** Federal income tax withheld because I had **NO** tax liability **AND**
- This year I expect a refund of **ALL** Federal income tax withheld because I expect to have **NO** tax liability.

If you meet both conditions, write "EXEMPT" here . . . . ▶ | **7** |

Under penalties of perjury, I certify that I am entitled to the number of withholding allowances claimed on this certificate, or I am entitled to claim exempt status.

Employee's signature
(Form is not valid
unless you sign it) ▶ *Aubrey Bird*

Date ▶ 4/4/03

8 Employer's name and address (Employer: Complete lines 8 and 10 only if sending to the IRS.)	**9** Office code (optional)	**10** Employer identification number
Sandra Bird		

Cat. No. 10220Q

4.125   3³⁰   12.375   34.2.375

29

Complete the following activity.

EMPLOYEE EARNINGS RECORD
for the Quarter Ended *March 31, 20—*

Howard
Mr. Wilcox's
910 Holly Drive
Binghamton NY 13905

EMPLOYEE NO.:	45	MARITAL STATUS:	Married
POSITION:	Manager	ALLOWANCES:	3
RATE OF PAY:	$15.00	SSN:	123-45-6790

PAY PERIOD		EARNINGS			DEDUCTIONS					ACCUMULATED EARNINGS	
PAY NO.	ENDED	REGULAR	OVERTIME	TOTAL	FEDERAL INCOME TAX	FICA	HEALTH INSURANCE	OTHER	TOTAL DEDUCTIONS	NET PAY	YEAR TO DATE
1	1-15	1200 00		1200 00	89 00	91 80	50 00	15 00	245 80	954 20	1200 00
2	1-31	1200 00	70 00	1270 00	98 00	97 16	50 00	15 00	260 16	1009 84	2470 00
3	2-15	1200 00		1200 00	89 00	91 80	50 00	15 00	245 80	954 20	3670 00
4	2-28	1200 00		1200 00	89 00	91 80	50 00	15 00	245 80	954 20	4870 00
5	3-15	1200 00	70 00	1270 00	98 00	97 16	50 00	15 00	260 16	1009 84	6140 00
6	3-31	1200 00		1200 00	89 00	91 80	50 00	15 00	245 80	954 00	7340 00
	Totals	7200 00	140 00	7340 00	552 00	561 52	300 00	90 00	1503 52	5836 48	

4.3 The Employee Earnings Record above shows regular and overtime earnings for six semi-monthly pay periods in January, February and March of the current year for Mr. Howard Wilcox.

a. Complete the upper portion of the form using the following information:

Address:	910 Holly Drive, Binghamton, NY 13905.
Employee number:	45
Marital Status:	Married
Allowances:	3
Rate of Pay:	$15.00
Social Security No.:	123-45-6790
Position:	Manager

b. Calculate Mr. Wilcox's earnings, deductions and accumulated earnings for each of the six pay periods shown on this form. Use the tax tables on page 31–34 to find the employee's federal withholding amount. Mr. Wilcox's employer combines Social Security and Medicare (7.65% of total earnings each pay period).

Regular deductions each pay period: Health insurance – $50.00
U.S. Savings Bonds – $15.00

c. Total the columns to check your work when finished.

NOTE: The tax tables on the following pages may be cut out of the booklet to make completion of certain exercises easier.

SINGLE Persons- SEMIMONTHLY Payroll Period
(For Wages Paid in 2000)

If the wages are-		And the number of withholding allowances claimed is-										
At least	But less than	0	1	2	3	4	5	6	7	8	9	10
		The amount of income tax to be withheld is-										
$0	$115	0	0	0	0	0	0	0	0	0	0	0
115	120	1	0	0	0	0	0	0	0	0	0	0
120	125	2	0	0	0	0	0	0	0	0	0	0
125	130	3	0	0	0	0	0	0	0	0	0	0
130	135	3	0	0	0	0	0	0	0	0	0	0
135	140	4	0	0	0	0	0	0	0	0	0	0
140	145	5	0	0	0	0	0	0	0	0	0	0
145	150	6	0	0	0	0	0	0	0	0	0	0
150	155	6	0	0	0	0	0	0	0	0	0	0
155	160	7	0	0	0	0	0	0	0	0	0	0
160	165	8	0	0	0	0	0	0	0	0	0	0
165	170	9	0	0	0	0	0	0	0	0	0	0
170	175	9	0	0	0	0	0	0	0	0	0	0
175	180	10	0	0	0	0	0	0	0	0	0	0
180	185	11	0	0	0	0	0	0	0	0	0	0
185	190	12	0	0	0	0	0	0	0	0	0	0
190	195	12	0	0	0	0	0	0	0	0	0	0
195	200	13	0	0	0	0	0	0	0	0	0	0
200	205	14	0	0	0	0	0	0	0	0	0	0
205	210	15	0	0	0	0	0	0	0	0	0	0
210	215	15	0	0	0	0	0	0	0	0	0	0
215	220	16	0	0	0	0	0	0	0	0	0	0
220	225	17	0	0	0	0	0	0	0	0	0	0
225	230	18	0	0	0	0	0	0	0	0	0	0
230	235	18	1	0	0	0	0	0	0	0	0	0
235	240	19	2	0	0	0	0	0	0	0	0	0
240	245	20	2	0	0	0	0	0	0	0	0	0
245	250	21	3	0	0	0	0	0	0	0	0	0
250	260	22	4	0	0	0	0	0	0	0	0	0
260	270	23	6	0	0	0	0	0	0	0	0	0
270	280	25	7	0	0	0	0	0	0	0	0	0
280	290	26	9	0	0	0	0	0	0	0	0	0
290	300	28	10	0	0	0	0	0	0	0	0	0
300	310	29	12	0	0	0	0	0	0	0	0	0
310	320	31	13	0	0	0	0	0	0	0	0	0
320	330	32	15	0	0	0	0	0	0	0	0	0
330	340	34	16	0	0	0	0	0	0	0	0	0
340	350	35	18	0	0	0	0	0	0	0	0	0
350	360	37	19	2	0	0	0	0	0	0	0	0
360	370	38	21	3	0	0	0	0	0	0	0	0
370	380	40	22	5	0	0	0	0	0	0	0	0
380	390	41	24	6	0	0	0	0	0	0	0	0
390	400	43	25	8	0	0	0	0	0	0	0	0
400	410	44	27	9	0	0	0	0	0	0	0	0
410	420	46	28	11	0	0	0	0	0	0	0	0
420	430	47	30	12	0	0	0	0	0	0	0	0
430	440	49	31	14	0	0	0	0	0	0	0	0
440	450	50	33	15	0	0	0	0	0	0	0	0
450	460	52	34	17	0	0	0	0	0	0	0	0
460	470	53	36	18	1	0	0	0	0	0	0	0
470	480	55	37	20	2	0	0	0	0	0	0	0
480	490	56	39	21	4	0	0	0	0	0	0	0
490	500	58	40	23	5	0	0	0	0	0	0	0
500	520	60	42	25	7	0	0	0	0	0	0	0
520	540	63	45	28	10	0	0	0	0	0	0	0
540	560	66	48	31	13	0	0	0	0	0	0	0
560	580	69	51	34	16	0	0	0	0	0	0	0
580	600	72	54	37	19	2	0	0	0	0	0	0
600	620	75	57	40	22	5	0	0	0	0	0	0
620	640	78	60	43	25	8	0	0	0	0	0	0
640	660	81	63	46	28	11	0	0	0	0	0	0
660	680	84	66	49	31	14	0	0	0	0	0	0
680	700	87	69	52	34	17	0	0	0	0	0	0
700	720	90	72	55	37	20	2	0	0	0	0	0
720	740	93	75	58	40	23	5	0	0	0	0	0
740	760	96	78	61	43	26	8	0	0	0	0	0
760	780	99	81	64	46	29	11	0	0	0	0	0
780	800	102	84	67	49	32	14	0	0	0	0	0
800	820	105	87	70	52	35	17	0	0	0	0	0
820	840	108	90	73	55	38	20	3	0	0	0	0

Page 44

Federal Income Tax Withholding

MARRIED Persons- SEMIMONTHLY Payroll Period
(For Wages Paid in 2000)

If the wages are-		And the number of withholding allowances claimed is-										
At least	But less than	0	1	2	3	4	5	6	7	8	9	10
		The amount of income tax to be withheld is-										
$0	$270	0	0	0	0	0	0	0	0	0	0	0
270	280	1	0	0	0	0	0	0	0	0	0	0
280	290	2	0	0	0	0	0	0	0	0	0	0
290	300	4	0	0	0	0	0	0	0	0	0	0
300	310	5	0	0	0	0	0	0	0	0	0	0
310	320	7	0	0	0	0	0	0	0	0	0	0
320	330	8	0	0	0	0	0	0	0	0	0	0
330	340	10	0	0	0	0	0	0	0	0	0	0
340	350	11	0	0	0	0	0	0	0	0	0	0
350	360	13	0	0	0	0	0	0	0	0	0	0
360	370	14	0	0	0	0	0	0	0	0	0	0
370	380	16	0	0	0	0	0	0	0	0	0	0
380	390	17	0	0	0	0	0	0	0	0	0	0
390	400	19	1	0	0	0	0	0	0	0	0	0
400	410	20	3	0	0	0	0	0	0	0	0	0
410	420	22	4	0	0	0	0	0	0	0	0	0
420	430	23	6	0	0	0	0	0	0	0	0	0
430	440	25	7	0	0	0	0	0	0	0	0	0
440	450	26	9	0	0	0	0	0	0	0	0	0
450	460	28	10	0	0	0	0	0	0	0	0	0
460	470	29	12	0	0	0	0	0	0	0	0	0
470	480	31	13	0	0	0	0	0	0	0	0	0
480	490	32	15	0	0	0	0	0	0	0	0	0
490	500	34	16	0	0	0	0	0	0	0	0	0
500	520	36	19	1	0	0	0	0	0	0	0	0
520	540	39	22	4	0	0	0	0	0	0	0	0
540	560	42	25	7	0	0	0	0	0	0	0	0
560	580	45	28	10	0	0	0	0	0	0	0	0
580	600	48	31	13	0	0	0	0	0	0	0	0
600	620	51	34	16	0	0	0	0	0	0	0	0
620	640	54	37	19	2	0	0	0	0	0	0	0
640	660	57	40	22	5	0	0	0	0	0	0	0
660	680	60	43	25	8	0	0	0	0	0	0	0
680	700	63	46	28	11	0	0	0	0	0	0	0
700	720	66	49	31	14	0	0	0	0	0	0	0
720	740	69	52	34	17	0	0	0	0	0	0	0
740	760	72	55	37	20	2	0	0	0	0	0	0
760	780	75	58	40	23	5	0	0	0	0	0	0
780	800	78	61	43	26	8	0	0	0	0	0	0
800	820	81	64	46	29	11	0	0	0	0	0	0
820	840	84	67	49	32	14	0	0	0	0	0	0
840	860	87	70	52	35	17	0	0	0	0	0	0
860	880	90	73	55	38	20	3	0	0	0	0	0
880	900	93	76	58	41	23	6	0	0	0	0	0
900	920	96	79	61	44	26	9	0	0	0	0	0
920	940	99	82	64	47	29	12	0	0	0	0	0
940	960	102	85	67	50	32	15	0	0	0	0	0
960	980	105	88	70	53	35	18	0	0	0	0	0
980	1,000	108	91	73	56	38	21	3	0	0	0	0
1,000	1,020	111	94	76	59	41	24	6	0	0	0	0
1,020	1,040	114	97	79	62	44	27	9	0	0	0	0
1,040	1,060	117	100	82	65	47	30	12	0	0	0	0
1,060	1,080	120	103	85	68	50	33	15	0	0	0	0
1,080	1,100	123	106	88	71	53	36	18	1	0	0	0
1,100	1,120	126	109	91	74	56	39	21	4	0	0	0
1,120	1,140	129	112	94	77	59	42	24	7	0	0	0
1,140	1,160	132	115	97	80	62	45	27	10	0	0	0
1,160	1,180	135	118	100	83	65	48	30	13	0	0	0
1,180	1,200	138	121	103	86	68	51	33	16	0	0	0
1,200	1,220	141	124	106	89	71	54	36	19	1	0	0
1,220	1,240	144	127	109	92	74	57	39	22	4	0	0
1,240	1,260	147	130	112	95	77	60	42	25	7	0	0
1,260	1,280	150	133	115	98	80	63	45	28	10	0	0
1,280	1,300	153	136	118	101	83	66	48	31	13	0	0
1,300	1,320	156	139	121	104	86	69	51	34	16	0	0
1,320	1,340	159	142	124	107	89	72	54	37	19	2	0
1,340	1,360	162	145	127	110	92	75	57	40	22	5	0
1,360	1,380	165	148	130	113	95	78	60	43	25	8	0
1,380	1,400	168	151	133	116	98	81	63	46	28	11	0
1,400	1,420	171	154	136	119	101	84	66	49	31	14	0

Federal Income Tax Withholding

SINGLE Persons- WEEKLY Payroll Period
(For Wages Paid in 2000)

If the wages are-		And the number of withholding allowances claimed is-										
At least	But less than	0	1	2	3	4	5	6	7	8	9	10
		The amount of income tax to be withheld is-										
$0	$55	0	0	0	0	0	0	0	0	0	0	0
55	60	1	0	0	0	0	0	0	0	0	0	0
60	65	2	0	0	0	0	0	0	0	0	0	0
65	70	2	0	0	0	0	0	0	0	0	0	0
70	75	3	0	0	0	0	0	0	0	0	0	0
75	80	4	0	0	0	0	0	0	0	0	0	0
80	85	5	0	0	0	0	0	0	0	0	0	0
85	90	5	0	0	0	0	0	0	0	0	0	0
90	95	6	0	0	0	0	0	0	0	0	0	0
95	100	7	0	0	0	0	0	0	0	0	0	0
100	105	8	0	0	0	0	0	0	0	0	0	0
105	110	8	0	0	0	0	0	0	0	0	0	0
110	115	9	1	0	0	0	0	0	0	0	0	0
115	120	10	2	0	0	0	0	0	0	0	0	0
120	125	11	3	0	0	0	0	0	0	0	0	0
125	130	11	3	0	0	0	0	0	0	0	0	0
130	135	12	4	0	0	0	0	0	0	0	0	0
135	140	13	5	0	0	0	0	0	0	0	0	0
140	145	14	6	0	0	0	0	0	0	0	0	0
145	150	14	6	0	0	0	0	0	0	0	0	0
150	155	15	7	0	0	0	0	0	0	0	0	0
155	160	16	8	0	0	0	0	0	0	0	0	0
160	165	17	9	1	0	0	0	0	0	0	0	0
165	170	17	9	1	0	0	0	0	0	0	0	0
170	175	18	10	2	0	0	0	0	0	0	0	0
175	180	19	11	3	0	0	0	0	0	0	0	0
180	185	20	12	4	0	0	0	0	0	0	0	0
185	190	20	12	4	0	0	0	0	0	0	0	0
190	195	21	13	5	0	0	0	0	0	0	0	0
195	200	22	14	6	0	0	0	0	0	0	0	0
200	210	23	15	7	0	0	0	0	0	0	0	0
210	220	25	17	8	0	0	0	0	0	0	0	0
220	230	26	18	10	2	0	0	0	0	0	0	0
230	240	28	20	11	3	0	0	0	0	0	0	0
240	250	29	21	13	5	0	0	0	0	0	0	0
250	260	31	23	14	6	0	0	0	0	0	0	0
260	270	32	24	16	8	0	0	0	0	0	0	0
270	280	34	26	17	9	1	0	0	0	0	0	0
280	290	35	27	19	11	3	0	0	0	0	0	0
290	300	37	29	20	12	4	0	0	0	0	0	0
300	310	38	30	22	14	6	0	0	0	0	0	0
310	320	40	32	23	15	7	0	0	0	0	0	0
320	330	41	33	25	17	9	1	0	0	0	0	0
330	340	43	35	26	18	10	2	0	0	0	0	0
340	350	44	36	28	20	12	4	0	0	0	0	0
350	360	46	38	29	21	13	5	0	0	0	0	0
360	370	47	39	31	23	15	7	0	0	0	0	0
370	380	49	41	32	24	16	8	0	0	0	0	0
380	390	50	42	34	26	18	10	2	0	0	0	0
390	400	52	44	35	27	19	11	3	0	0	0	0
400	410	53	45	37	29	21	13	5	0	0	0	0
410	420	55	47	38	30	22	14	6	0	0	0	0
420	430	56	48	40	32	24	16	8	0	0	0	0
430	440	58	50	41	33	25	17	9	1	0	0	0
440	450	59	51	43	35	27	19	11	3	0	0	0
450	460	61	53	44	36	28	20	12	4	0	0	0
460	470	62	54	46	38	30	22	14	6	0	0	0
470	480	64	56	47	39	31	23	15	7	0	0	0
480	490	65	57	49	41	33	25	17	9	0	0	0
490	500	67	59	50	42	34	26	18	10	2	0	0
500	510	68	60	52	44	36	28	20	12	3	0	0
510	520	70	62	53	45	37	29	21	13	5	0	0
520	530	71	63	55	47	39	31	23	15	6	0	0
530	540	73	65	56	48	40	32	24	16	8	0	0
540	550	75	66	58	50	42	34	26	18	9	1	0
550	560	78	68	59	51	43	35	27	19	11	3	0
560	570	81	69	61	53	45	37	29	21	12	4	0
570	580	84	71	62	54	46	38	30	22	14	6	0
580	590	87	72	64	56	48	40	32	24	15	7	0
590	600	89	74	65	57	49	41	33	25	17	9	1

Page 36

33

MARRIED Persons- WEEKLY Payroll Period
(For Wages Paid in 2000)

If the wages are-		And the number of withholding allowances claimed is-										
At least	But less than	0	1	2	3	4	5	6	7	8	9	10
		The amount of income tax to be withheld is-										
$0	$125	0	0	0	0	0	0	0	0	0	0	0
125	130	1	0	0	0	0	0	0	0	0	0	0
130	135	1	0	0	0	0	0	0	0	0	0	0
135	140	2	0	0	0	0	0	0	0	0	0	0
140	145	3	0	0	0	0	0	0	0	0	0	0
145	150	4	0	0	0	0	0	0	0	0	0	0
150	155	4	0	0	0	0	0	0	0	0	0	0
155	160	5	0	0	0	0	0	0	0	0	0	0
160	165	6	0	0	0	0	0	0	0	0	0	0
165	170-	7	0	0	0	0	0	0	0	0	0	0
170	175	7	0	0	0	0	0	0	0	0	0	0
175	180	8	0	0	0	0	0	0	0	0	0	0
180	185	9	1	0	0	0	0	0	0	0	0	0
185	190	10	1	0	0	0	0	0	0	0	0	0
190	195	10	2	0	0	0	0	0	0	0	0	0
195	200	11	3	0	0	0	0	0	0	0	0	0
200	210	12	4	0	0	0	0	0	0	0	0	0
210	220	14	6	0	0	0	0	0	0	0	0	0
220	230	15	7	0	0	0	0	0	0	0	0	0
230	240	17	9	0	0	0	0	0	0	0	0	0
240	250	18	10	2	0	0	0	0	0	0	0	0
250	260	20	12	3	0	0	0	0	0	0	0	0
260	270	21	13	5	0	0	0	0	0	0	0	0
270	280	23	15	6	0	0	0	0	0	0	0	0
280	290	24	16	8	0	0	0	0	0	0	0	0
290	300	26	18	9	1	0	0	0	0	0	0	0
300	310	27	19	11	3	0	0	0	0	0	0	0
310	320	29	21	12	4	0	0	0	0	0	0	0
320	330	30	22	14	6	0	0	0	0	0	0	0
330	340	32	24	15	7	0	0	0	0	0	0	0
340	350	33	25	17	9	1	0	0	0	0	0	0
350	360	35	27	18	10	2	0	0	0	0	0	0
360	370	36	28	20	12	4	0	0	0	0	0	0
370	380	38	30	21	13	5	0	0	0	0	0	0
380	390	39	31	23	15	7	0	0	0	0	0	0
390	400	41	33	24	16	8	0	0	0	0	0	0
400	410	42	34	26	18	10	2	0	0	0	0	0
410	420	44	36	27	19	11	3	0	0	0	0	0
420	430	45	37	29	21	13	5	0	0	0	0	0
430	440	47	39	30	22	14	6	0	0	0	0	0
440	450	48	40	32	24	16	8	0	0	0	0	0
450	460	50	42	33	25	17	9	1	0	0	0	0
460	470	51	43	35	27	19	11	3	0	0	0	0
470	480	53	45	36	28	20	12	4	0	0	0	0
480	490	54	46	38	30	22	14	6	0	0	0	0
490	500	56	48	39	31	23	15	7	0	0	0	0
500	510	57	49	41	33	25	17	9	1	0	0	0
510	520	59	51	42	34	26	18	10	2	0	0	0
520	530	60	52	44	36	28	20	12	4	0	0	0
530	540	62	54	45	37	29	21	13	5	0	0	0
540	550	63	55	47	39	31	23	15	7	0	0	0
550	560	65	57	48	40	32	24	16	8	0	0	0
560	570	66	58	50	42	34	26	18	10	2	0	0
570	580	68	60	51	43	35	27	19	11	3	0	0
580	590	69	61	53	45	37	29	21	13	5	0	0
590	600	71	63	54	46	38	30	22	14	6	0	0
600	610	72	64	56	48	40	32	24	16	8	0	0
610	620	74	66	57	49	41	33	25	17	9	1	0
620	630	75	67	59	51	43	35	27	19	11	2	0
630	640	77	69	60	52	44	36	28	20	12	4	0
640	650	78	70	62	54	46	38	30	22	14	5	0
650	660	80	72	63	55	47	39	31	23	15	7	0
660	670	81	73	65	57	49	41	33	25	17	8	0
670	680	83	75	66	58	50	42	34	26	18	10	2
680	690	84	76	68	60	52	44	36	28	20	11	3
690	700	86	78	69	61	53	45	37	29	21	13	5
700	710	87	79	71	63	55	47	39	31	23	14	6
710	720	89	81	72	64	56	48	40	32	24	16	8
720	730	90	82	74	66	58	50	42	34	26	17	9
730	740	92	84	75	67	59	51	43	35	27	19	11

STATE INCOME TAX WITHHOLDING TABLES
Semi-Monthly (twice per month) Payroll Period
(effective January 1, 2000)

4.2% of gross pay should be withheld if no exemptions are claimed.

If wages are		and the number of withholding exemptions claimed is ----										
at least	but less than	0	1	2	3	4	5	6	7	8	9	10
		the amount of income tax withheld is ----										
0	8	0.17										
8	16	0.50										
16	24	0.84										
24	32	1.18										
32	40	1.51										
40	48	1.85										
48	56	2.18										
56	64	2.52										
64	72	2.86										
72	80	3.19										
80	88	3.53										
88	96	3.86										
96	104	4.20										
104	112	4.54										
112	120	4.87										
120	128	5.21	0.14									
128	136	5.54	0.47									
136	144	5.88	0.81									
144	152	6.22	1.15									
152	160	6.55	1.48									
160	168	6.89	1.82									
168	176	7.22	2.15									
176	184	7.56	2.49									
184	192	7.90	2.83									
192	200	8.23	3.16									
200	208	8.57	3.50									
208	216	8.90	3.83									
216	224	9.24	4.17									
224	232	9.58	4.51									
232	240	9.91	4.84									
240	248	10.25	5.18	0.11								
248	256	10.58	5.51	0.44								
256	264	10.92	5.85	0.78								
264	272	11.26	6.19	1.12								
272	280	11.59	6.52	1.45								
280	288	11.93	6.86	1.79								
288	296	12.26	7.19	2.12								
296	304	12.60	7.53	2.46								
304	312	12.94	7.87	2.80								
312	320	13.27	8.20	3.13								
320	328	13.61	8.54	3.47								
328	336	13.94	8.87	3.80								
336	344	14.28	9.21	4.14								
344	352	14.62	9.55	4.48								
352	360	14.95	9.88	4.81								

-14-

STATE INCOME TAX WITHHOLDING TABLES
Semi-Monthly (twice per month) Payroll Period
(effective January 1, 2000)
4.2% of gross pay should be withheld if no exemptions are claimed.

| If wages are | | and the number of withholding exemptions claimed is ---- | | | | | | | | | | |
at least	but less than	0	1	2	3	4	5	6	7	8	9	10
		the amount of income tax withheld is ----										
360	368	15.29	10.22	5.15	0.08							
368	376	15.62	10.55	5.48	0.41							
376	384	15.96	10.89	5.82	0.75							
384	392	16.30	11.23	6.16	1.09							
392	400	16.63	11.56	6.49	1.42							
400	408	16.97	11.90	6.83	1.76							
408	416	17.30	12.23	7.16	2.09							
416	424	17.64	12.57	7.50	2.43							
424	432	17.98	12.91	7.84	2.77							
432	440	18.31	13.24	8.17	3.10							
440	448	18.65	13.58	8.51	3.44							
448	456	18.98	13.91	8.84	3.77							
456	464	19.32	14.25	9.18	4.11							
464	472	19.66	14.59	9.52	4.45							
472	480	19.99	14.92	9.85	4.78							
480	488	20.33	15.26	10.19	5.12	0.05						
488	496	20.66	15.59	10.52	5.45	0.38						
496	504	21.00	15.93	10.86	5.79	0.72						
504	512	21.34	16.27	11.20	6.13	1.06						
512	520	21.67	16.60	11.53	6.46	1.39						
520	528	22.01	16.94	11.87	6.80	1.73						
528	536	22.34	17.27	12.20	7.13	2.06						
536	544	22.68	17.61	12.54	7.47	2.40						
544	552	23.02	17.95	12.88	7.81	2.74						
552	560	23.35	18.28	13.21	8.14	3.07						
560	568	23.69	18.62	13.55	8.48	3.41						
568	576	24.02	18.95	13.88	8.81	3.74						
576	584	24.36	19.29	14.22	9.15	4.08						
584	592	24.70	19.63	14.56	9.49	4.42						
592	600	25.03	19.96	14.89	9.82	4.75						
600	608	25.37	20.30	15.23	10.16	5.09	0.02					
608	616	25.70	20.63	15.56	10.49	5.42	0.35					
616	624	26.04	20.97	15.90	10.83	5.76	0.69					
624	632	26.38	21.31	16.24	11.17	6.10	1.03					
632	640	26.71	21.64	16.57	11.50	6.43	1.36					
640	648	27.05	21.98	16.91	11.84	6.77	1.70					
648	656	27.38	22.31	17.24	12.17	7.10	2.03					
656	664	27.72	22.65	17.58	12.51	7.44	2.37					
664	672	28.06	22.99	17.92	12.85	7.78	2.71					
672	680	28.39	23.32	18.25	13.18	8.11	3.04					
680	688	28.73	23.66	18.59	13.52	8.45	3.38					
688	696	29.06	23.99	18.92	13.85	8.78	3.71					
696	704	29.40	24.33	19.26	14.19	9.12	4.05					
704	712	29.74	24.67	19.60	14.53	9.46	4.39					
712	720	30.07	25.00	19.93	14.86	9.79	4.72					

-15-

STATE INCOME TAX WITHHOLDING TABLES
Semi-Monthly (twice per month) Payroll Period
(effective January 1, 2000)

4.2% of gross pay should be withheld if no exemptions are claimed.

If wages are		and the number of withholding exemptions claimed is ----										
at least	but less than	0	1	2	3	4	5	6	7	8	9	10
		the amount of income tax withheld is ----										
720	728	30.41	25.34	20.27	15.20	10.13	5.06					
728	736	30.74	25.67	20.60	15.53	10.46	5.39	0.32				
736	744	31.08	26.01	20.94	15.87	10.80	5.73	0.66				
744	752	31.42	26.35	21.28	16.21	11.14	6.07	1.00				
752	760	31.75	26.68	21.61	16.54	11.47	6.40	1.33				
760	768	32.09	27.02	21.95	16.88	11.81	6.74	1.67				
768	776	32.42	27.35	22.28	17.21	12.14	7.07	2.00				
776	784	32.76	27.69	22.62	17.55	12.48	7.41	2.34				
784	792	33.10	28.03	22.96	17.89	12.82	7.75	2.68				
792	800	33.43	28.36	23.29	18.22	13.15	8.08	3.01				
800	808	33.77	28.70	23.63	18.56	13.49	8.42	3.35				
808	816	34.10	29.03	23.96	18.89	13.82	8.75	3.68				
816	824	34.44	29.37	24.30	19.23	14.16	9.09	4.02				
824	832	34.78	29.71	24.64	19.57	14.50	9.43	4.36				
832	840	35.11	30.04	24.97	19.90	14.83	9.76	4.69				
840	848	35.45	30.38	25.31	20.24	15.17	10.10	5.03				
848	856	35.78	30.71	25.64	20.57	15.50	10.43	5.36	0.29			
856	864	36.12	31.05	25.98	20.91	15.84	10.77	5.70	0.63			
864	872	36.46	31.39	26.32	21.25	16.18	11.11	6.04	0.97			
872	880	36.79	31.72	26.65	21.58	16.51	11.44	6.37	1.30			
880	888	37.13	32.06	26.99	21.92	16.85	11.78	6.71	1.64			
888	896	37.46	32.39	27.32	22.25	17.18	12.11	7.04	1.97			
896	904	37.80	32.73	27.66	22.59	17.52	12.45	7.38	2.31			
904	912	38.14	33.07	28.00	22.93	17.86	12.79	7.72	2.65			
912	920	38.47	33.40	28.33	23.26	18.19	13.12	8.05	2.98			
920	928	38.81	33.74	28.67	23.60	18.53	13.46	8.39	3.32			
928	936	39.14	34.07	29.00	23.93	18.86	13.79	8.72	3.65			
936	944	39.48	34.41	29.34	24.27	19.20	14.13	9.06	3.99			
944	952	39.82	34.75	29.68	24.61	19.54	14.47	9.40	4.33			
952	960	40.15	35.08	30.01	24.94	19.87	14.80	9.73	4.66			
960	968	40.49	35.42	30.35	25.28	20.21	15.14	10.07	5.00			
968	976	40.82	35.75	30.68	25.61	20.54	15.47	10.40	5.33	0.26		
976	984	41.16	36.09	31.02	25.95	20.88	15.81	10.74	5.67	0.60		
984	992	41.50	36.43	31.36	26.29	21.22	16.15	11.08	6.01	0.94		
992	1000	41.83	36.76	31.69	26.62	21.55	16.48	11.41	6.34	1.27		
1000	1008	42.17	37.10	32.03	26.96	21.89	16.82	11.75	6.68	1.61		
1008	1016	42.50	37.43	32.36	27.29	22.22	17.15	12.08	7.01	1.94		
1016	1024	42.84	37.77	32.70	27.63	22.56	17.49	12.42	7.35	2.28		
1024	1032	43.18	38.11	33.04	27.97	22.90	17.83	12.76	7.69	2.62		
1032	1040	43.51	38.44	33.37	28.30	23.23	18.16	13.09	8.02	2.95		
1040	1048	43.85	38.78	33.71	28.64	23.57	18.50	13.43	8.36	3.29		
1048	1056	44.18	39.11	34.04	28.97	23.90	18.83	13.76	8.69	3.62		
1056	1064	44.52	39.45	34.38	29.31	24.24	19.17	14.10	9.03	3.96		
1064	1072	44.86	39.79	34.72	29.65	24.58	19.51	14.44	9.37	4.30		
1072	1080	45.19	40.12	35.05	29.98	24.91	19.84	14.77	9.70	4.63		

-16-

30.74

Extra Form:

PAYROLL REGISTER for the Semimonthly Payroll Period Ended _____

NO.	EMPLOYEE DATA			EARNINGS			DEDUCTIONS					NET PAY
	NAME	MARITAL STATUS	EXEMP.	REGULAR	OVERTIME	TOTAL	FEDERAL INCOME TAX	FICA	GROUP HEALTH INSURANCE	OTHER	TOTAL DEDUCTIONS	AMOUNT